FINAL TABLE

FINAL TABLE

A Winning Poker Approach
from a WSOP Champion

JONATHAN DUHAMEL

Translated by Christina Palassio

ECW Press

Published originally under the title: *Cartes sur table* © 2011, Les Éditions de L'Homme, division de Groupe Sogides Inc., filiale de Quebecor Media Inc. (Montréal, Québec, Canada)
Translation © Christina Palassio, 2012

Published by ECW Press
2120 Queen Street East, Suite 200, Toronto, Ontario, Canada M4E 1E2
416-694-3348 / info@ecwpress.com

Library and Archives Canada Cataloguing in Publication

Duhamel, Jonathan, 1987–
Final table : a winning poker approach from a WSOP
champion / Jonathan Duhamel.

Translation of: Cartes sur table.
ISBN 978-1-77041-113-5
Also issued as: 978-1-77090-316-6 (PDF); 978-1-77090-317-3 (ePub)

1. Duhamel, Jonathan, 1987–.   2. Poker.   3. Poker players.

I. Title.

GV1250.2.D83A313 2012   795.412092   C2012-902644-1

Cover and text design: Tania Craan
Production and typesetting: Troy Cunningham
Printing: Berryville Graphics   1   2   3   4   5

The publication of Final Table has been generously supported by the Ontario Arts Council, an agency of the Government of Ontario. We also acknowledge the financial support of the Government of Canada through the Canada Book Fund for our publishing activities. The marketing of this book was made possible with the support of the Ontario Media Development Corporation.

Printed and bound in the United States

Table of Contents

Foreword

I first met Jonathan in January 2011. We were playing poker together at the same table, and that's where I was introduced both to his style of play and to a really good guy. Jonathan is a determined young man. But what impressed me most about him were his lack of pretension and his desire to build up a social network of friends and allies around him with whom to exchange knowledge.

I believe that those are the qualities that make Jonathan an excellent poker player. He has meticulously perfected his style of play and respectfully integrated himself into the community, and he acknowledges his successes with humility.

And he has had great success. As a fellow Quebecker, I'm proud of him. You can't help but be proud of someone who, no matter the field, can set himself apart, persevere and inspire others.

Being at the top of the game requires great discipline and a lot of passion. You have to be willing to make sacrifices, be open to continuing to learn, and dream — always dream. That's the way it is in business, in the arts, in sports, and that's also how it is for poker players.

Ever since that first meeting, I've had the pleasure of following Jonathan's professional and personal progress. He easily maintains that winning approach founded on respect, inspiration and sharing. This book is a testament to that fact. His desire to share his experience in order to inspire both pros and amateurs is proof of a great maturity and an understanding of the values that guide great players.

I learned more about Jonathan through this book, and I can't wait to join him again at a poker table, where camaraderie feeds the joy you feel when you live each of life's moments to the fullest.

Guy Laliberté
Founder of Cirque du Soleil

Introduction

On November 9, 2010, I became the first Canadian to win the Main Event of the World Series of Poker, the world's most famous and most lucrative no-limit Texas Hold'em tournament, which that year played host to 7,319 players from 92 different countries. I came home with $8,944,310.

That didn't change the world, but . . .

Most people would think I was lying if I told them that I haven't been on cloud nine since the win. I'm proud that I beat the best players in the world to take that title, but I still feel like my accomplishments in poker are few. In poker, just like in sports, business, art or politics, the real challenge is consistency. You're only ever judged by your last performance. So you have to learn how to keep a good head on your shoulders, whether you're winning or losing.

My win in the Main Event of the WSOP brought me a lot of satisfaction, of course, but it also made popular some ideas about me that are contrary to my ethics and values, which are founded on respect and hard work. For example, many people said that I'd dropped out of my business program at the Université de Québec à Montréal in order to become a professional poker player. But nothing could be further from the truth.

In the summer of 2008, as I was heading into the third year of my degree, I decided that finance wasn't what I wanted to do with my life. I'd given it a lot of thought. I decided to take a year off to travel and think about my next step. In Québec, people don't always understand that decision, and many liken it to dropping out. But in England and Scandinavia, taking a gap year to travel and get some real-world experience is completely normal, even encouraged. The thought of earning a living playing poker had nothing to do with that decision.

It's true that I was already playing online poker at that point, and making decent money at it. But my first real encounter with the poker world only occurred at the end of 2008. That fall, a friend of mine told me that a high-profile tournament — the Main Event of the European Poker Tour — was taking place in Prague that December. I decided to register and to take advantage of being in Europe to travel around for a few weeks afterwards. I finished tenth out of 570 players, missing the final table by a hair, and took home a pot of €42,000 (almost US$55,000), which ensured my financial stability for the year.

Then, in 2009, I played in a few tournaments, but I didn't make any real money. As my sabbatical wrapped up that summer, I still hadn't chosen a new career path. But thanks to the Prague tournament, I had enough money to see me through the foreseeable future. So I decided to take another year off.

It was in 2010 that things really changed. I played in several U.S. tournaments, making a profit in three of them and taking home more than $60,000 before I registered for the WSOP Main Event that was set to start in Las Vegas in May. On July 17, the last day of the preliminary round, I was one of the nine remaining players who would go on to make up the final table in four months. That meant I was guaranteed to take home at least US$800,000. When the competition started up again, I would be in the lead with more than a third of the chips, and I had a pretty good chance of winning.

It goes without saying that at that point, there was no way I was going to go back to school only to leave again in November. And the rest, as they say, is history.

Poker is an exciting and intense game in which luck plays a much smaller role than many people think. You have to practice for hours and hours and constantly want to best yourself in order to win on a regular basis. You also need talent and skill. Some of those skills you're born with. Others you can acquire over the years. It's the latter category that I'll talk about in this book. Some of those skills involve math, while others involve a keen sense of observation. Others have to do with how well you know yourself and other people. I've somewhat arbitrarily pegged the number of skills at 18. Some overlap and intersect, but one thing's for sure: during a tournament, each skill comes into play and makes the difference between a win and a loss.

This isn't a how-to book, nor is it a collection of tricks and shortcuts for quick and easy improvement. There is no easy money in poker. Players lured by the promise of easy money are quickly disappointed: you won't see those players at the professional level. Like in most fields, it's through talent, hard work, determination and a well thought-out strategy that you get the best results.

I've had the pleasure to rub elbows with and play against some of the world's best players over the past few years. I learned a lot from them and continue to do so. All of those champions, from Daniel Negreanu to Phil Ivey, Phil Hellmuth and Allen Cunningham, possess the 18 qualities described in this book. You just can't win without them.

1

Passion

"Lots of pros aren't passionate about what they do, and it shows. I love poker. I love everything about it. It's the best game in the world. I'm always trying to improve my game and to move up. I have a huge advantage over those of my opponents who only play because it's their job." — **Phil Ivey**

Everything starts with passion . . .

That said, this kind of passion isn't one that I seemed predestined to have. We often assume that children inherit their parents' quirks and qualities, even though it's seldom the case. But neither poker nor any other betting game ever made it past the doorstep of our house while I was growing up. My father, Luc Duhamel, who has worked as a machinist at Pratt and Whitney for the past 30 years, and my mother, Johanne Grenier, a teller at the Desjardins credit union in Boucherville, taught me from a very young age that money doesn't grow on trees . . . or on cards.

My parents instilled in me the values of hard work, self-discipline and integrity early on. They taught by example. At 13, I was spending most of my summer picking strawberries on farms in the Montérégie region. At 16, I was putting in more than 30 hours a week in the stockroom of the Provigo grocery store in Boucherville. I've never been afraid of work, be it physical or intellectual. That's still true today. It wasn't until I was in my early twenties that the idea that I might be able to make a lot of money playing poker started to germinate in my mind.

♠

I remember very clearly the first time I played poker. I was 15 or 16. It was a Friday night in Boucherville, and I was hanging out with some friends in a friend's basement watching TV. A totally typical night, one like so many others from that time in my life. And that's when my initiation took place. The older brother of the friend whose house we were in came down to hang out with us and suggested we play a game of five-card draw. We ended up playing all night, without any stakes — just for fun.

I don't know if you can use the term "love at first sight" to describe such unremarkable circumstances, but let's just say that I was immediately taken by the game. It was simple and complex all at the same time. It had strategy, suspense, doubt and excitement, and it involved calculations that appealed to my mathematical side. And then there was the luck factor. The game might not have been so appealing if it wasn't for that key element. It was like a game of chess with a dose of chance thrown in. The combination of all of those elements led me to fall in love with poker, and it's a feeling that has never wavered.

Soon after that night, I started playing several nights a week with some kids from the neighborhood, but always for very small stakes. Betting made the game more complete and thrilling, but it wasn't the heart of why we liked to play. That had more to do with the game itself. We started out playing five-card draw and then moved on to all sorts of other variations. Initially, Texas Hold'em didn't appeal to us much because we thought it didn't offer much action. We preferred a variation where we could bluff more, which seemed to open up the game and make it a lot more exciting. But as we got better, Texas Hold'em became our favorite variation. Hold'em requires much more skill and strategy than the traditional five-card game, partly because five of your seven cards are community cards that are shared by all players. And the fact that it's easier to play and to understand makes it easier to find other people to play. That's why it's become so popular over the past decade.

I think back fondly on that period of learning and discovery. I spent a lot of time on the internet in those days, seeking out information, adding to my body of knowledge, studying strategy and, eventually, playing at free-to-play tables. At some point, one of my friends put down $20 online, and I watched as he played it. After that, I started betting small amounts, and participating in online tournaments in which I had a moderate amount of success. I think I've proven by now that I have the qualities necessary to get to the top of the game, but you'd be wrong to think it all happened by magic. It isn't magic for anyone. I lost more than I won, but I was constantly improving and, more importantly, my thirst for knowledge and my passion for the game always remained strong.

♠

Passion for the game can take many different forms. For people who are motivated by risk, that passion can extend to any game of chance, from roulette to blackjack to backgammon. But that passion can also begin and end with poker, as it does with me. Or it can be conflated with the allure of easy money, which, I should stress, doesn't make for a very long career. And then there are people who have a real and ongoing infatuation with poker but who never feel the need to scale up their study of the game.

One thing's for sure though: anyone who's ever had real success at poker started out feeling that passion for the game, and they still feel it in one way or another. It's the trigger, the first step and the prerequisite for moving forward and winning in a consistent way.

> **ACCORDING TO JONATHAN:** "I believe passion is a prerequisite for success — it's the fuel for the fire. You can work to keep it lit, but you can't create it if there isn't already a spark. That's what makes it such an invaluable asset."

The passion I'm referring to here is for the game of poker itself. I'm not talking about a lust for money or fame or victory, even though they tend to be the goal of most competitions. I'm also not talking about the enthusiasm of the casual player who likes to play but doesn't feel like investing in the game. What I'm talking about is an unquenchable thirst for knowledge and self-improvement. The foundation of that passion is humility, an awareness of one's weaknesses and shortcomings and the unshakeable belief in the possibility for improvement that comes from devoting time and effort to the game and being willing to make all the necessary sacrifices. Passion isn't the sole factor, but everything else follows from it. It's what compels you to do everything it takes to move forward, to acquire discipline, self-control, a good sense of observation and all the other skills I'll talk about in this book.

In this respect, the poker player's passion is no different from the passion that drives people to excel in other fields. Think of hockey players who start off with a love for the game and the skills to advance, but who have to put in years of practice and sacrifice to get to the NHL. Think of those young players who at 16, or even sometimes younger, leave their families and friends to go play in the junior leagues, where they spend hours every week traveling on buses from one small town to the next, bound by a rigorous routine and required to put in the effort that's needed to excel in an extremely competitive environment every single day. And they all do it without any guarantee they'll make it to the NHL. The thing that makes these kids willing to give up the regular life of a teenager is passion for the sport, and the hope that they might one day be part of an elite group.

I'm thinking here too of Guy Laliberté — founder of Cirque du Soleil — a man I'm lucky enough to know and whose company I enjoy immensely. Here's a guy who turned his dreams into a global empire, creating a market from scratch while he was at it — a man who's not afraid to see his passions and talents straight through to the end. His dedication is obvious not only in the Cirque du Soleil empire, but also in his skills as a poker player (which are much better than the average player's), and in the self-discipline he needed in order to train for his trip to space in October 2009.

Another person who comes to mind is Georges St-Pierre, an exceptionally intelligent man who has taken a lot of risks to follow his passion for mixed martial arts. That passion has become much more than a career; it's a way of life that involves lengthy and challenging daily training sessions and a philosophy that's both contemporary and of the past. Georges lives the life of a warrior. When he's in the ring, it's more important to him to put in a good effort and to meet his own expectations than it is to win the fight. I think his attitude is instructive for anyone who wants to live their passion in a healthy and productive way.

There's no doubt in my mind that anyone who's ever succeeded in their field has felt that spark of passion from which excellence springs. We often think of passion as a messy, all-consuming emotion that can lead to destructive excesses. It's easy to imagine someone being overwhelmed by passion if they're not careful. For me though, passion is a fuel, a source of positive energy that I use as a motivator to achieve my goal. That goal is to be the best. In every hand, in every game, in every tournament.

As Phil Ivey said in the quotation that starts this chapter, the challenge is to maintain that beginner's passion for the game. Appearances can be deceiving: it's really not as easy as it seems. It's not natural to maintain the same level of interest in the same task for many years. And money can change a lot of things. Passion is often compromised when profit becomes the primary goal. The minute poker stops being a hobby and starts becoming the way you make a living, there's always a chance it can become more rote. Whether you're playing a game or in a tournament, sitting down to a poker table can end up feeling like just another day at the office. When you become a full-time player and start spending 50 or 60 hours a week at a table or in front of a computer screen, you risk becoming blasé. And then there's the greater stress of playing at higher levels, which can wear down even the most seasoned players.

Lots of players lose their passion along the way. It's a risk anyone who's considering throwing themselves into professional poker should seriously think about. I've known lots of passionate players who lost their spark when they tried to make poker the center of both their life and their livelihood. That kind of situation can affect both your life balance and your performance. The intense passion a poker player feels and the success he experiences make him want to do nothing but play, which then threatens his inner balance and his initial passion. It's a cruel irony. Poker starts out as a passion, but it often also becomes a place of refuge. You look forward to it all day long and it becomes an oasis from your daily responsibilities. But how do you stay balanced when poker becomes a responsibility instead of a hobby? Many professional players take up another sport or hobby. With Johnny Chan, it's photography. Daniel Negreanu plays golf. Chris Ferguson dances. Me, I still love to play hockey — even though I'm an average player at best — and to watch Canadiens games. And though I like it, it's a passion that remains far inferior to poker.

Of course, your passion for poker changes when you start winning more often, playing for higher and higher stakes and comparing yourself to some of the world's best players. You still like the game, but other factors start to come into play, like making sure you're still moving up in spite of stiffer competition and increasing risk. It becomes a matter of continuing to accept bigger challenges, which, though difficult, also motivates. Every time you get to the next rung in the poker hierarchy, you're immediately compelled to continue to the next step, to stay on top. Since poker is constantly changing, staying in the same place really means you're moving backwards. The things that make me a good player today won't be enough to guarantee me a win tomorrow. There are always new challenges.

The other thing that ends up mattering a lot more when you get to elite poker circles — and this is also probably true in most fields and careers — is the esteem of the public, and especially of your peers. When pros that I respect and admire — people like Daniel Negreanu, Jason Mercier, Barry Greenstein and Vanessa Rousso — make me feel like I'm part of the club, it makes me extremely proud and motivates me to try my best to stay at their level of play.

When I won the 2010 World Series of Poker, I not only became a poker ambassador for the year, I also had to prove that my win wasn't a fluke, that I really was part of the elite, even if my odds of winning the 2011 tournament were very low. Thankfully, I placed first in a tournament in Deauville, France, in January 2011 and took home €200,000 (about US$260,000). I also did well in a few subsequent tournaments, most of them in the U.S., which helped me deal with the pressure that's inevitably placed on a champion after a big win. Given those outcomes, it's tough not to stay addicted to poker.

There are other situations in which passion for the game can become temporarily dulled. Losing streaks and financial losses can greatly affect a player's self-confidence and his desire to play. They're situations every player deals with. Amateurs tend to take a break in order to rebuild their confidence. Pros, on the other hand, tend to play through the losing streak as best they can — while trying to limit their losses, of course — in order to rediscover their love of the game and their success at the table.

You shouldn't put too much pressure on yourself during a losing streak. You have to keep paying attention to what's happening around the table, stay focused and continue making good decisions and playing in a methodical way. You also have to spend the hands you're not playing watching your opponents and familiarizing yourself with their strategy so you can get an edge on them. Things may not sort themselves out right away, but if you keep playing the game like it should be played, they'll eventually fall back into place.

Everything starts with passion, but that doesn't mean it's easy to maintain. It disappears and reappears. It's largely subject to success at the table and to the laws of probability. But you have to ensure that it doesn't ever disappear completely, in large part because it's so closely linked to your self-confidence. And the last thing you need when you're playing poker is a lack of confidence.

2

Self-confidence

"I've always had confidence, but I never let my

ego get to the point that I think I'm the superstar,

because I know that ego has destroyed many a

poker career." — **Jim Boyd**

The minute I sit down at a poker table, whether with friends or in a WSOP tournament, I'm keyed up. I'm there to win, not there to play a part or to fight over a few dollars. I'm there to take control of that table. End of story. Things don't always turn out the way I want, of course, but you can't play poker at a high level without having a lot of confidence in yourself, your skills and your ability to beat your opponents.

Here too you can draw lots of comparisons between poker and sports, or poker and other areas of life. When Roger Federer walks onto the court, he's not going to be satisfied with anything less than a win. When Céline Dion gets on stage at Caesars Palace, she's not thinking about the possibility that she could make a mistake or miss a note. When Steve Jobs launched a new version of the iPad, the possibility of commercial failure likely never crossed his mind.

You can't succeed if you doubt yourself. You become shy, fearful, hesitant. You become paralyzed by the fear of losing everything. As they say, fear is a poor advisor. Fear prevents you from thinking clearly and making good decisions. That can be particularly dangerous in poker, a game where you have to make a series of decisions based on an established strategy and incomplete information gleaned from a combination of your own cards, the community cards, the laws of probability and the betting habits of other players.

Your self-confidence is closely linked to how good your opponents are — or how good you think they are. Every time you move up a rung on the ladder you feel a bit of self-doubt, because you know that you're about to play against better players. So you ask yourself: Is now the time to move up? Am I at the level? Am I about to get schooled? It's normal to ask yourself these questions, but you can't dwell on them if you want to keep moving forward.

It's easy to feel intimidated in poker. I remember when I started playing against well-established players, players I'd often seen on TV, that I admired, and whose careers I followed closely. I wouldn't say that I was ever distracted to the point where I lost my composure, but I was definitely impressed. It felt a bit like being a rookie NHL goalie and seeing Alexander Ovechkin coming at you on a breakaway for the first time. During my first few encounters with marquee players, I tried as much as possible to avoid making eye contact, to forget who they were, to convince myself that no matter how much I admired them, they were opponents like any others and I could beat them.

After I won a few hands, I realized that their fame didn't give them as great an advantage over me as many believed. They were great players, sure, but I quickly realized that it was no accident that I was at the same table as them, playing in the same leagues. After all, there are 52 cards in a deck, and each player gets the same number of cards. The rest depends on the decisions you make. That's the way you have to approach the game: without arrogance and without hang-ups.

While moving up in the poker hierarchy may bring with it additional pressure and moments of self-doubt, it also really helps to build confidence. When you start playing against better and better players and continue to succeed, you realize that no matter how good your opponents are, you know how to make the right decisions.

It's important to remember, however, that there are two different kinds of self-confidence in poker. There's the kind that comes out in the short-term, during a game or a tournament, and that ebbs and flows depending on the situation. And then there's the kind that grows over a longer period of time and that corresponds to a state of mind, to the feeling a player gets when he's had a prolonged series of successes.

For example, a player's position at the table can have a huge influence on his short-term confidence, especially if he's the first player to act and a player he finds intimidating is seated on his left. Poker players have to make decisions based on incomplete information, so the last player to bet has the greatest advantage, since he has the most information. He's seen who folded, who bet and how much; he's had the opportunity to observe his opponents and thus has a greater chance of accurately evaluating where he stands.

I remember having Phil Galfond, an intimidating opponent who I respect a lot, sitting on my left for a whole day during the 2010 WSOP. Phil is a very smart player, and he's also very aggressive, especially when he can tell you're scared of him. I had a nightmare of a day because of him. He raised constantly, which kept throwing me off-balance. He quickly noticed that my confidence was wavering and took full advantage of the situation. And because I was playing really tight, I was never able to get the upper hand. It's a good example of a situation where my confidence was rattled and I ended up just trying to control the damages. But it was only one day, and days like that rarely have lasting consequences. It's the long-term confidence that's much more important. That's what you want to hold on to, because that's what will help you win regularly and set yourself apart from other players.

It's easy to win when luck is on your side. The real challenge is winning when the cards are working against you. That's when you have to be in full control, have a good read on the game and make logical decisions that aren't influenced by emotion. You can only hold your own if you're feeling confident and the other players know it. But maintaining that confidence, especially when you're losing, requires strength of character. It's understandable to want to change course when things aren't working out, but that's exactly what you should never do. That's why the crises of confidence that arise during a downswing are some of a poker player's most difficult challenges.

Even the best players go through losing streaks of varying lengths. They know it's inevitable, because mathematical variance is so integral to the game. The problem is that poker players aren't machines. They're humans who react to poor results by questioning their skills and doubting themselves. Were my past successes due to luck instead of skill? Should I try a new strategy? Should I take more risks, or should I play more conservatively? That's when you get sucked into a vicious cycle and your confidence plummets so much that you no longer know if your losses are the result of a lack of competence or if they're simply due to a stroke of bad luck.

In poker jargon, that downward spiral is called being on tilt.

It's the worst thing that can happen to a player. Being on tilt refers to a situation where, whether out of disgust, anger or frustration, a player lets his emotions dictate his method of play instead of relying on reason and logic. This loss of control can manifest in several ways. Having lost a large bet, a player might become overly aggressive and start taking unnecessary risks in the hopes — usually imaginary — that he'll be able to make up for his losses. A different player will have a tendency to start playing more defensively, to play fewer hands and to be more conservative in his bets, which will keep him from raising the stakes and winning big pots. In both cases, players abandon their usual strategy because of a loss of confidence. But by changing tactics so obviously, you're sending your opponents the message that you're not in control of your game — that you're panicked and vulnerable. And you can be sure that they won't pass up the opportunity to take advantage of your weakness. Tilt is a poker player's worst enemy, because it keeps him from thinking clearly and making the right decisions. You have to be able to identify it as it's happening and to control it. Otherwise, it can cost you.

One of the reasons it's so difficult to remain confident when you're playing poker is that, unlike in most other types of competitions, luck plays a determining role in the results. Athletes go through slumps that affect their confidence and their concentration. But even though you often hear excuses like "we just weren't getting the bounces," athletes know that the milliseconds or millimeters that make the difference between a homerun and a foul ball, between a goal and a puck that goes off the goalpost, between a birdie and a bogey, have more to do with physical conditioning and coordination than they do with luck.

The poker player, on the other hand, knows he has to dally with chance, but he can't consider it a determining factor. In other words, you can't let the fact that you've lost the past 15 or 20 hands influence the way you'll play the next one. Easier said than done? Absolutely. But remember: unlike humans, cards have no memory.

How do you get over a crisis of confidence in poker? The simple answer is that you start winning again. It's obvious, but it's precisely the problem: since your lack of self-confidence is affecting your game, you have fewer chances to do what it takes to win and, as a result, you risk prolonging your losing streak. There's no magic formula. Some players stop playing for a while to let the storm blow over. Others try to bring their confidence levels back up by placing smaller bets for a while. Since there's less pressure, they figure they'll be less obsessed by the fear of losing and they'll play in a more rational and disciplined manner. Many others go back to playing online. The reason there are an increasing number of good poker players on the planet is unarguably because of the internet, which has made the game so much more accessible and has allowed thousands of people to learn the basics, to practice and to improve. That's what happened in my case, and it's the same for many of the elite players I know.

Online poker can be a great tool for rebuilding your confidence. You can play for small stakes or for free, which means you can also improve for free. Most importantly, you can start winning again after a slump, which will help rebuild your confidence. It's a simple question of mathematical variance. Before the internet, there was a limit to the number of hands a player could play, since all games were played in person. With online poker, a single player can now play millions of hands in a year. You can even play several hands at the same time, which is what I often do. And variance guarantees that, over a long period of time, a high-caliber player will inevitably make a profit. That's why so many players turn to online poker when they need to rebuild their confidence.

♥

Self-confidence is so important when it comes to poker that it's difficult to imagine having too much. But there's a nuance here that I should stress. In poker, as in life, you should never let confidence lead you to underestimate your opponent, regardless of their level of skill, either real or imagined.

Confidence may be essential to winning consistently, but believing yourself to be a superior player — when you're on a winning streak, for example — can lead the inexperienced player into dangerous situations. An excess of confidence alters your judgment as much as fear does, and it can lead to the same results. You become less vigilant, you play more hands, you ask fewer questions before placing a bet and you take more uncalculated risks. In other words, you become lazy and start to think you don't have to improve, that everything's easy from here on in. That kind of arrogance can be extremely dangerous. A player who's too sure of himself will blame his losses on bad luck instead of a bad play . . . and then he'll just keep losing.

It's important to remember that while confidence is important, it has to be built on a solid foundation that includes an ability to calculate probabilities based on the information at hand: your hole cards, the flop, the turn and the river.

It was the third day of the main event of the 2010 WSOP. Things were going pretty well, even though my stack (which is the sum you have on hand at a given moment during a game or a tournament) was about the same size as everyone else's. I had a good read on the table and on each of the players, and I really felt like I was squeezing the most value out of every hand. In other words, I was growing my stack without taking too many risks. I was where I wanted to be in the tournament and I was feeling confident.

Around dinnertime, an active player I think is pretty good raises before the flop in middle position. I have off-suit A-K in the small blind and I re-raise. He calls and the flop comes KH-9S-6S. I bet about 60% of the pot, and he raises three times my bet. I don't want to re-raise because if he goes all-in, I'll probably be coming from behind, and I don't want to play such a huge pot at this stage of the tournament. Still, I don't feel like I can fold my hand. I call.

The turn comes 4C. I check and, to my surprise, so does he. The river comes 7C, and I bet about half the pot, figuring that I probably have the better hand and hoping I'll get paid off by his weaker hand — any pair between a 9 and K. He could even call with a pair of 9s or a pair of 7s he got on the river, if he'd been playing a straight draw hand with a 7 and 8.

To my surprise, he raises 3.75 times the value of my bet, forcing me to commit more than half of the total value of my stack. I'm now faced with a decision that's as difficult as it is crucial to the rest of the game.

My opponent could have three 6s or three 9s, or he could've even drawn three 7s on the river. But the board is also full of missed draws. Spades are still incomplete, and 7s and 8s have only ended up in a pair. I also know he's probably thinking I have a pair of kings or another pair between 9 and K. If he's drawing dead, I know the only way to win the pot is to call his bluff by raising like he did. Even though there are many hands that could make me lose, I figure my chances of being ahead are pretty good. Having considered all these possibilities, I decide to call.

My opponent flips over J-10 — a failed flush and straight draw. I take home a huge pot that boosts my confidence, which is already fairly high. Had I not built up that confidence over the preceding hours, I might've been more hesitant to call.

3

Knowing Your Numbers

"A good player has to have solid math skills. He has to know his percentages, has to know when he has a pair that he has a one in eight chance of getting trips. You've got to understand the math of poker before you can think about playing for money."

— Patrick Bruel

When I'm playing poker, I sometimes feel like my brain is a hard drive that stores all the facts I need to make the right decisions. Not just probability calculations, but also each player's style, the size of the stacks, the size of the bets, which player has just come off a big win and who's just lost a lot of chips, who's looking like they might be on tilt and who might be feeling overly confident. The volume of information you can accumulate in a game is practically limitless, and each piece of information could end up being the difference between a win and a loss.

Each player has his own way of managing the data he collects over the course of a poker game. Some, like Chris Ferguson, who has a Ph.D. in computer science, prioritize mathematical data. Others, like Daniel Negreanu, rely more on their ability to read their opponents. Others are more intuitive, but you realize they still base their decisions on logic and get good results. And in the end, that's all that counts.

Lots of people think that you have to have *Rain Man*–like math skills and a phenomenal memory to be a poker champion. You obviously don't need a doctorate to excel at poker, but it's true that math is a big part of the game, given your constant need to rely on probability calculations.

I don't pretend to have Chris Ferguson's math skills, but I've always been pretty good at math. As far back as I can remember, it was my favorite subject at school, the class I did the best in and that motivated me to want to learn more. That skill serves me well today. Beyond being good with numbers, I think I've also been successful in applying the meticulousness, the care and the self-discipline to poker that I always demonstrated in my math classes and when I studied finance in university.

◆

To play poker well, you need to know a few basic mathematical facts that aren't very hard to master.

Let's start with the fact that in Texas Hold'em, there are 1,326 different possible combinations of hole cards, which are the two first hidden cards you're dealt, the ones that will determine in large part if you bet or not. Each of those starting combinations carries an expected value that varies depending on the number of players and what's dealt going forward. Only a small percentage of starting hands are worth playing and, again, not at any cost.

For example, suppose I have pocket jacks going in. It's a great starting hand that gives me more than a three out of four chance of winning the pot if there's only one other player with an unknown hand at the table. I can play this hand with confidence. But say I have those same pocket jacks while sitting at a 10-player table — my chances of winning fall to about 20%, and I can only bet if the circumstances justify it. The decision is trickier than it would be in a heads-up game. The more players there are, the greater the chances that one of my opponents has a good hand.

Knowing the probabilities associated with each hand, both before and after the flop, allows me to have a clearer picture of my situation and to better control my game. When you stop to think about the millions of combinations that are possible in bridge, you realize that poker isn't all that complicated. You can venture far into the range of possibilities if you have an advanced mathematical mind, but you don't need to have a very high level of skill in order to be able to make sensible and lucrative decisions.

That said, there's one thing that sets a champion apart from your average player, and that's the ability to quickly and efficiently calculate the potential for profit in a certain situation, otherwise known as the "pot odds." The pot odds are the ratio between the amount you have to put into a pot and the amount you can get out of it, taking into consideration the cards you have in your hand. That ratio can tell you, on a strictly monetary level, whether it's worth investing in a pot.

Let's say I have AS-9S, and the community cards are the KS-6S-10H-2D. There's $25 in the pot. I only have one opponent, and he goes all-in with his remaining $15. What are my chances of winning the pot if I decide to call his $15 bet in a situation where there's only one card still to be dealt?

First, I have to determine the cost-benefit ratio in order to figure out if my investment will be profitable. In this case, it would cost me $15 to win $40, which is a ratio of 37.5% (15/40). I then have to identify which cards can give me a win, given that my analysis leads me to believe that my opponent has a pair of kings. In this case, it'd be any spade or ace left in the deck. There are 13 spades in a deck. I have two in my hand and there are two on the table. So there are nine left. In addition, there are four aces in a deck and I have one. So there are three left. Which means there are 12 cards that can give me a winning hand. In poker, we call those cards "outs."

Now I have to evaluate my profit chances based on these cards. I know six of 52 cards: the two I have in my hand and the four that are on the board. 46 are unknown. My chances of winning are 12 over 46, or 26%. (A simpler and less precise way of calculating your chances is to multiply the number of outs by two. That would give us 24% in this case, which is pretty close.) If my chances of winning (26%) are less than the potential profit of my investment, I should fold.

Of course, if it's not an all-in situation, the calculations become more complicated. In that case, you have to evaluate the implied pot odds — the amount of money you can win if you hit one of your outs. Implied pot odds are especially important in no-limit games and games where the size of the stacks is likely to be big.

Let's say I have QS-5S, and the flop turns up KS-6S-10D. Same as in the previous example, the pot is $25, except this time my opponent doesn't go all-in. Instead, he bets $15 from a $200 stack. My stack is worth $240. Again, I have to choose whether to invest the $15. Like in the previous example, there's a 25% chance that a winning card will be dealt, or a 37.5% cost-benefit ratio. Does logic dictate I should fold again? Not necessarily, because the calculations aren't the same in this situation, given that other bets might increase the size of the pot. I now need to evaluate both my chances of winning the pot and the possibility that additional amounts might be added to it. If a winning card comes out on the turn or on the river, I could win more than the $40 that's currently in play.

On the other hand, what happens if my card doesn't come out on the turn and my opponent bets again? I'll have to pay again, but there'll only be one card left to deal. And, if I get my flush to the queen but my opponent makes his to the ace, he could take my whole stack.

As you can see, calculating implied odds requires more than mathematical ability: you also have to know your opponent, as that knowledge will largely dictate your decision. If I'm playing against an aggressive opponent, I'm pretty sure he'll bet at the turn and at the river. If I call, there's a good chance the value of the pot will increase. If I'm playing against a more timid opponent, it still might be a good idea to raise since he might fold if I seem confident. But if he's playing tight, he likely won't invest again. And if I'm pretty sure he'll be running scared if a spade comes out, then the amount of the pot probably won't grow even if I get my out, so I should fold.

By mastering the calculation of pot odds and implied odds, a player adds a new weapon in his arsenal that allows him to move to another level. And don't let yourself be put off by these calculations: the same odds repeat again and again, so you'll quickly learn how to master them as soon as you're dealt your cards.

♦

Another mathematical element that can greatly influence how a game unfolds, and whether or not you decide to play a hand, is the number of players at the table. When there are 10, as in the previous example, there's a much greater chance that one of them will have a good hand, which means you're more likely to proceed with caution and be more patient. In those situations, players tend to be more selective when it comes to the hands they play, often choosing to play only one hand for every six or seven dealt. In a heads-up game, on the other hand, you can be a bit more aggressive, bluff more and play up to nine out of 10 hands.

As I've tried to explain, knowing your numbers isn't just about recording mathematical data and performing complex calculations. The poker champion analyzes every bit of information he can collect that might help him to make the right decisions. The more information you're able to collect, put into context and treat effectively, the better player you'll become in the long run.

Remember that over the course of a game, the smallest detail can become grist for the mill and help you to make regular profits. That's why the computer in your head has to be going full throttle at all times, like a hamster on a wheel. You have to be aware of every sign and gesture that's happening at the table, and your opponents' attitudes and reactions. Who are they? What are their goals in this tournament?

How is each player perceived by the others? Who is on tilt? Who is tired? How have they played their hands so far? I'll discuss the importance of knowing your opponents in a later chapter. For now, let's just say that it's important to treat every sign in a poker match as a piece of data that you need to absorb and analyze in order to play the best game possible.

ACCORDING TO JONATHAN: "Having a hard drive in my head allows me to evaluate every variable that comes into play when I'm making a decision. A good part of a player's success is due to intuition, but it's the ability to transition to 'math mode' that allows you to maintain a superior level of play."

But beware! The math tool is a step forward, but it also contains a very real risk: that of manipulating the numbers to say something they're not. A novice player may have subconsciously already made a decision, but instead of analyzing all the information at hand in order to act logically, he may only pay attention to the data that supports his decision. It's crucial to be aware of this danger.

That said, being able to rapidly accumulate and process information also leads to a certain consistency and automatic responses that can help you manage stress. There's an interesting parallel to be drawn here with the kinds of sports that require intense concentration. Take golf, a sport where the smallest break in concentration can have disastrous consequences. The professional golfer also has a hard drive in his head that tells him which club to choose, how to position his body and which stroke to use based on the distance of the hole, the direction and speed of the wind, the slope of the course and the obstacles between him and the green. To stay free of tension, the pro golfer also establishes a strict routine that helps him concentrate and avoid distractions. Looking at the ball, taking position, warm-up swings, breathing — this process, akin to a ritual, helps him control his emotions and stay in his comfort zone.

In addition to all the numbers and calculations and the importance of being aware of everything that's happening at the table, the computer in my head also has to have a global understanding of the entire tournament and the match that's underway, and to be able to see beyond the present moment as much as possible, a bit like in chess. You need a keen sense of observation to acquire that awareness. The computer is also useful in keeping an inventory of the many varieties of information that will help you make your decisions.

In addition to probability calculations, top-ranked players also take into consideration facets of the game of poker that, while not directly related to math or technique, can become crucial over the course of a game. For example, I know most of the players that I'm likely to meet during a tournament. I've played against them and I remember our previous encounters, and they remember me too. What happened the last time Michael Mizrachi and I played together? Who had the upper hand? How was he playing? What attitude did he have? Was he playing aggressively, or was he being careful? Did he bluff a lot? Did I notice a weakness in his game, or was I the one who played badly on a few hands? And, if so, why? I'm sure he's performing a similar analysis. Even if I've never played against a certain player, I still know his reputation; I've analyzed a few of his games and I have a decent understanding of his style. He's probably studied some of my games too.

What you need to remember is that at the highest levels of poker, as in most individual sports, the players are about equal when it comes to technical skill. Each player has mastered probability math and can accurately analyze his position at any given moment during a game or tournament. So something else makes the difference: the luck of the draw, of course, but also the powers of observation, psychology and your ability to read your opponents.

It's important to keep in mind that even though the mastery of math is first and foremost, the computer in your head doesn't have only one job to do. The calculator must also be equipped with radar that can detect even the most minute bits of information that are being traded around the table. It's an ongoing task that requires your complete attention and doesn't allow for lapses in concentration.

4

Getting in the Zone

"When you're in the zone, you're acting on
automatic pilot and something from deep within you
is coordinating your skills, turning tough decisions
into instinctive athletic artwork, and guiding you
effortlessly to victory." — **Doyle Brunson**

You may have noticed while watching televised poker championships that many players hide behind large sunglasses. Chris Moneymaker does it, and so do Chris Ferguson, Scotty Nguyen, Vanessa Rousso and many others. Some believe wearing sunglasses gives them a menacing air that allows them to intimidate their opponents, while others use sunglasses as a way to hide their eyes and their emotions, which makes it easier to maintain a poker face. That's probably true for a good number of players. Sunglasses also act as a screen between you and other players, and allow you to maintain the sacred territory of your private thoughts, to stay in the zone, that safe place where your mind can focus on one single thing: the game at hand.

When you're in the zone, it feels like you're in full control of your senses, that you're able to absorb even the most minor details, that you can anticipate your opponents' plays, that you're prepared for any eventuality. In other words, when you're in the zone, you think you're controlling the table.

Sustained concentration is crucial in poker, both when you're playing a hand and when you're not. In no-limit games especially, the slightest distraction can be very expensive.

Nobody's safe from lapses in concentration. Not even the best players. Ask Phil Ivey, one of the top two or three players in the world, a man who's known for his exceptional ability to stay focused. During the 2009 WSOP, with only 24 players remaining out of 6,484 registrants, he folded a spade flush to Jordan Smith's two pairs (aces and queens), not realizing that he had the better hand. That mistake can only be explained by a flagrant lapse of concentration, and it cost Ivey a $2.18 million pot. He still qualified for the final table and placed fourth in the tournament, but who knows what might've happened if a player of his caliber had shown up at that table with an additional $2 million worth of chips in his stack.

♣

I'm convinced that my ability to maintain a high level of concentration played an important role in my win at the 2010 WSOP. Every day, I'd put on a hoodie with the colors of my sponsor, Pokerstars.net, and I'd pull the hood over my head at a slight angle. The edges of the hood acted like blinders, and meant that the only thing I saw were the cards and chips in the center of the table and the players around it. I took advantage of the hands I didn't play to watch my opponents, but the hood helped me forget everything that wasn't part of the game, avoid distractions and maintain a high degree of concentration throughout the day.

I've never wanted to be in the zone more than during the final duel against John Racener during the Main Event of the 2010 WSOP. One of us would become the world champion, and the other would miss out on the chance of a lifetime.

Everything threatened to make me lose my concentration. First, there was the crowd and the cameras, both unusual to me. Then, there was pressure to win — in other words, the challenge not to crack under pressure — given that I was up in chips and widely favored to win.

In the minds of the spectators, all I had to do was finish Racener off. It was only a matter of time. In my mind, it was a whole other ball game. One mistake and the tides could turn. More than ever before, I had to stay focused and stay in the zone in order to be able to play the best poker I was capable of.

In the middle of our duel, Racener gets 4S-2D, and I check with JD-4C. The flop comes 3S-JC-9D. I check. Racener bets and I call. 4D comes out on the turn, which ensures that I'll win the hand, even though I can't be sure of it in the moment. I check, and so does Racener.

10S comes out on the river and doesn't change much. I bet and, to my surprise, Racener raises. I could've gotten carried away at that moment, with victory so close at hand. Yet, objectively, going all-in wouldn't have been the best play. It would've meant taking a big risk against a tight player. If he called, I could've still been beat.

In spite of my excitement, and of the cameras and my supporters going wild, I keep my cool and go on playing what I think is the best play, which is to call. I win the hand, stay in the zone and finish the job a few minutes later.

That hand may seem banal, but it's not easy to stay in

> control of your emotions and remain calm whatever the external conditions may be when you're facing the biggest challenge of your life.

Like many pro players, I listen to playlists I've made on my iPod during games. Let's just say there's no Led Zeppelin or Iron Maiden on my playlists, even though some players like listening to more aggressive types of music while in tournament mode. I prefer to listen to soft music at a low volume. It provides some background noise but still allows me to hear what's being said at the table, and it relaxes me and helps me concentrate.

Obviously, not every player shares my M.O. Some players think listening to music during a poker game distracts you from what's happening around the table and deprives you of important information your opponents might give away. Others think that players who listen to music slow down the game. (This is definitely true when a player is listening to very loud music.) It's up to each player to find the trick that helps them concentrate, play well and make the right decisions.

It really isn't easy to stay in the zone for many consecutive hours. A player can hammer away for the first 11 hours of a tournament day and increase his chips by 25% only to have his concentration lapse — whether because of fatigue, hunger or the simple wish to be done with it — in the final hour, make a bad decision and find himself in a bad situation. A small analytical mistake made before the flop can become significant when you get to the river. Given the consequences, it's important to take every possible measure to ensure an optimal level of concentration.

That's why, as a rule, you should never go near a poker table when you're stressed out, tired or on tilt. It's an easy rule to follow when you're playing online: you don't have to play if you don't feel up to it. However, elite players don't always have the luxury of skipping high-profile tournaments, not only because of the amounts at stake but because of their professional profile or sponsorship agreements. Tournaments like the World Series of Poker are spread out several days. They're veritable marathons that end up being both physically and mentally exhausting.

On a few occasions over the past few months, I've shown up to tournaments in a state of fatigue and without much interest in playing poker hour after hour. But when you're the world champion, you don't have much of a choice. So, regardless of the circumstances and the physical and mental pressure you're under, you have to take the steps necessary to find that zone again. For example, if I have to be at a tournament table at noon, I go to bed early the night before, I eat a solid breakfast and I really try to relax and mentally prepare myself for the long day ahead.

♣

In order to maintain your concentration, you have to be fully aware of the things that can distract you over the course of a game, and to know how to identify them as soon as they manifest themselves.

The first possible distraction is your immediate environment and your opponents. If one of them notices that you're easily distracted or intimidated, or that it's easy to get information out of you by talking a lot, you can bet that's what they'll try to do. Poker is a world without pity; don't ever forget it. Staying in the zone means remaining stone-faced in front of loudmouths who'll try to distract you. It's not always easy, especially for players who play mostly online. My opponents became very real when I ended up in the World Series tournaments. I had to be ready to face verbal interruptions, which can be very irritating and cause you to fly off the handle or leave your comfort zone.

It's not just the competition that can affect a player's concentration. It's also the fans. I'm sure a few of my opponents were annoyed when my supporters, dressed in the colors of the Montréal Canadiens, kept chanting *Olé Olé Olé* during the tail end of the 2010 WSOP.

But don't think that playing online means you're safe from distractions. Street noise, rowdy kids, the sound of the phone ringing, new email — all of those things can distract you and cause you to make mistakes and exit the zone.

Physical conditioning can also influence concentration. During the last World Series of Poker, I noticed that I was earning a big portion of my profits in the evening. That wasn't just because my opponents were tired; it was also due to their eating habits. When the dinner break came around 6 p.m., lots of players were starving and headed straight for a steak. It goes without saying that when they came back to the table, their bodies were focused on digestion, not concentration. To avoid being in that situation during a tournament, I always eat five light, high-protein snacks a day instead of three big meals. That way, I never get hunger pangs, and I'm never too full. Sitting at a poker table all day long can definitely make your body and your spirit stiff. To stay awake and alert during a tournament, I take full advantage of the 10-minute breaks we're given at regular intervals. I go outside to get some fresh air, I jump in place for a minute or two and I splash cold water on my face. I sometimes also go up to my room during the longer breaks so I can have a cold shower. They're simple yet effective tricks.

Another thing that can threaten your concentration — and this may seem strange given the sums of money at stake — is boredom. This comes up most often when things aren't going so well, when your interest in the tournament and your chances of coming out on top start to dwindle and the urge to throw in the towel starts to take over. That's a classic tilt situation, one that occurs when logic succumbs to emotion. You have to try to resist that kind of reaction if you want to win at poker with any sort of consistency. No matter the situation, you should always rely on logic when making a decision.

I'll mention it only in passing because it seems so obvious, but I feel I should insist fairly strongly on the following point: alcohol is the worst for taking you out of the zone. At a certain level of play, alcohol becomes enemy number one. Some people say that alcohol has a calming effect, and that may be true when it's consumed in moderation, but alcohol also slows your reflexes, which is the kiss of death in a game where you have to think and act quickly. It can also loosen your tongue and lead you to reveal information that could be useful to your opponents. And don't forget: alcohol is a depressant. It can ruin your mood almost immediately. That's when you fall prey to your emotions. Alcohol is guaranteed tilt. I never touch it during a tournament. It's my golden rule.

Like all the other weapons in a poker player's arsenal, concentration can improve over time. Beginners and occasional players shouldn't expect that their zone will be impenetrable from the beginning. Don't ask too much of yourself. Take it step by step. Trying to focus your attention everywhere at once can quickly become torture. Start off by watching one or two players at a time, especially those who seem the most skilled. How do they react to their starting hands? What ratio of hands do they play? In which situations and how often do they raise? You'll soon notice the computer in your brain increasing its ability to store information, and your field of observation getting bigger. It'll become second nature to you, so to speak, like being on auto-pilot.

Another way to stay focused is to follow a routine and give yourself dependable reference points that promote a certain psychological stability. Here I'm thinking of Johnny Chan, who places an orange in front of him on the table during tournaments. It started off as a way to cover up the smell of smoke back when people could smoke in most poker tournaments. Smoking is no longer allowed, but Johnny still keeps an orange near him as a good luck charm. I personally don't think he really believes in the magical properties of the citrus fruit. I think it's become part of a ritual that reassures him and helps him concentrate.

Throughout this chapter, I've stressed the importance of staying in the zone while playing a poker game. But it's just as important to be able to leave it once you've left the table, whether for just a moment or for the rest of the day.

It's exhausting to maintain constant mental and physical concentration over many consecutive hours. It's absolutely necessary to move on to other things once it's no longer required. You have to be able to empty your mind and encourage it to move to soothing and pleasant thoughts less demanding of your brain. If you can't do that, you risk becoming exhausted, unmotivated and disillusioned. Like in all kinds of competitions, you need to establish a balance between giving 100% when it counts and being able to relax once it's over.

It's not always easy. You have to have a lot of discipline.

5

Controlling Your Emotions

"The strong point in poker is never to lose your
temper, either with those you are playing with
or, more particularly, with the cards. There is no
sympathy in poker. Always keep cool. If you lose
your head you will lose all your chips."

— William J. Florence

It's nice to play a few rounds of low-stakes poker
with friends and family. You have fun in good company, you take each other for a ride and you don't
lose your shirt. High-profile tournaments, including
the World Series of Poker, are a whole different
story. I'm not afraid to say it: at that level, poker is
a merciless war in which you have to know how to
hide your arsenal, your strengths, your weaknesses
and especially your intentions.

In *The Art of War* — without a doubt the best trea-
tise on strategy every written, one that every poker
player would benefit from regularly consulting —
Sun Tzu wrote, in the sixth century B.C.: "A general
who doesn't know moderation, who is not master
of himself and who loses control at the first sign of

indignation or anger will always fall to his enemies. They will provoke him and set a thousand traps for him that his anger will keep him from recognizing and into which he will always fall." There's no better way to describe the threats to a player who allows himself to be ruled by his emotions.

God knows you go through a whole range of emotions over the course of a game or tournament. I remember a few moments during the 2010 WSOP when I thought my heart was going to beat right out of my chest! I'm sure most of the other players felt the same way. It's human to have emotions but, as a poker player, you need to be able to control them and keep them in check. If you can't, they'll affect your judgment and your way of playing. It's equally important to avoid showing other players what you're feeling, or you risk revealing vital information to your opponents and becoming an open book. That's how you lose control of your game.

I know most people may not consider poker a sport. After all, when you spend 12 hours a day sitting in one spot, moving only your hands over cards and chips, it's hard to pretend that you're doing any physical activity. But I believe poker is a mind sport. It's a mental battle that requires the same, if not more, commitment, attention and concentration as any physical sport. The difference is that when you're playing hockey, football or basketball, once you're immersed in the action, you're not expected to hide your emotions, unless it's to avoid penalties. The only exception to this comparison might be golf, where self-control plays a deciding role in the final outcome of a game.

When you make a decision in your day-to-day life, you often weigh what your head says against what your heart says — reason versus emotion. That's quite normal and, luckily, emotions win some of those private battles. Our relationships would be a lot more difficult if they didn't. In poker, though, there's no compromising. There's no room for your heart in the game. You have to be a robot. That's how it is.

In the long run, poker rewards rational decision-making. The more objective information I have and the better I am at analyzing it cold, the better my decisions will be and, in the end, the better my chances for profit. In that sense, emotions are like grains of sand that gum up the gears. They tend to take over when you're feeling upset, when you've lost a big pot or when you're on a losing streak. That's when doubt sets in, your analytical abilities dull and you start playing based on what you'd like reality to be instead of relying on the objective information around you. In other words, you leave the land of reason to bounce around the land of illusion.

What I'm talking about here is going on tilt, the insidious and destructive phenomenon I've alluded to several times already that is a central concept in poker. In their excellent book, *The Poker Mindset: Essential Attitudes for Poker Success*, Matthew Hilger and Ian Taylor write that tilt is "often (but not always) a regression of a player's game to a more basic level. He temporarily loses his self-discipline and control over his game and starts to make his decisions based on the way he'd like to play the game." Players usually go on tilt when things are going badly, but a winning streak can also cause a player to stop making rational decisions in reaction to an excess of confidence. In both cases emotion, not reason, dictates decision-making.

The rational nature of poker requires that you sacrifice the decisions you'd like to make at the expense of those that you *have* to make in order to maximize your profits. Like every player, I want to play more hands, to find out what the next card is, to bluff more often — in other words, to test my luck. But I know that if I behave that way, I'd lose most of the time. So I agree to play rationally and to consistently behave in a way that's counter to my natural inclinations in exchange for a single reward: monetary gain. Still, though, I can't control chance. There are times when, even if I've played my cards right, my recipe for rational play doesn't work. That's usually when the psychological break will occur: I feel like I respected the rules of the game, but with no reward. I start to feel like my cosignatory on the contract — fate, chance, luck or the poker gods — hasn't held up its end of the bargain. At that moment, I feel like I've been tricked, that I'm the victim of a great injustice. And, in a way, I want to try to get revenge by restoring my heart and intuition to their original positions. It's like I'm saying, "Starting now, I'm going to do what I want and whatever happens, happens."

Players who fall prey to being on tilt aren't stupid. They know that emotion has no place in the game, and that they'll only hurt themselves by making decisions that aren't based in logic. But they're frustrated and they need an outlet for their anger and disappointment.

The reality is that no one is safe from going on tilt. It's tough to control your emotions for hours at a time, no matter the circumstances. The important thing is to know when they start taking precedence over logic. When you start to feel the sense of injustice I described earlier, it's obvious you're no longer in control of yourself. You have to take that alarm bell seriously.

The first thing you need to know in order to remain in complete control of your emotions is that while players who make good decisions aren't always rewarded in the short term, they are always rewarded in the long term. Once you've understood and internalized that idea, you realize that decisions matter more than results. The money will follow sooner or later.

Losses are a part of a poker player's life. They're unavoidable, so you're better off just accepting them. That's the first step in controlling your emotions at the table. If you still feel like your downswing is affecting the way you're playing, you might want to skip a few hands. You might also choose only to play really strong starting hands like AA, KK, QQ and AK. That imposed discipline can help you to put things into perspective and to think more clearly. I can testify to the fact that my ability to control my emotions paid off during a tough moment at the 2010 WSOP.

Luck sometimes abandons you over eight days of competition. It happened to me on Day 5 of the Main Event of the 2010 WSOP.

In the middle of the day, a player with half my stack — and in a precarious position — raises before the flop from the cutoff seat. I turn over QS-QC on the button and triple his bet. He takes a moment to think and goes all-in. I call right away — a very easy decision.

He has 8S-8D.

The flop is AH-7C-5H and seems pretty harmless, but 9D on the turn means he has a real chance for a straight. There are four sixes and two eights that can give him a win, for a win probability of 13.6%. Unfortunately for me, 6S comes out on the river, and I lose half of my hard-won chips.

At that moment, I have every reason to lose control and go on tilt. But it's not my first tournament, and I'm familiar with its siren call. I'm strong, and I know how to control myself, even though my opponents don't know it yet. Several among them would be frustrated if they were in my shoes. So they can bet that I'm feeling that way at that moment.

A couple of hands later, I'm two seats to the right of the button and a player in early position makes a normal raise. Everyone folds. I have pocket Jacks, a perfect hand given the circumstances. Knowing that others think I'm on tilt, I decide to bet my whole stack, a reaction that's completely out of proportion with my opponent's move. That type of reaction is often a sign of frustration and weakness. I'm fully aware of the impression I'm giving off though, and I intend to use it to my advantage.

My strategy works perfectly. My opponent barely hesitates before calling with pocket 7s. No bad luck this time: I end up with the same stack I had three hands before.

There are two things about emotion you need to keep in mind when you're playing poker. One is internal and the other is external. The first thing you need to do is remain in control of yourself and not let emotions affect the decisions you make. The second is to camouflage what you're feeling to ensure your opponents can't tell what your intentions are. You could be thrilled or profoundly hopeless, but you have to seem indifferent and avoid displaying any reaction to what's going on around you. Players who can do this consistently — Phil Ivey is a master of this art form — are winners.

The need to hide your feelings goes much further than perfecting the poker face that's often associated (for good reasons) with top players. We should actually be talking about the poker body, because almost any part of your body can give you away during a match. Do my hands shake or do I blink a lot when I'm not happy with my cards? Do I pick up my cards too quickly? Do I throw in my chips too abruptly? When I lose a big pot, do I show a flash of impatience or am I too obvious about my displeasure? If I'm dealt a pair of aces, do I shift in my chair, almost imperceptibly, in a way that could reveal my hand? If I answer yes to any one of these questions, I'm vulnerable. My opponents will take advantage of my weaknesses sooner or later.

All good poker players are on the lookout for signs, idiosyncrasies or tics, which are usually called tells — those almost unnoticeable behaviors that can give away a lot about a player's strategy, their emotions or their intentions. We all have them. It's almost impossible to avoid them, because they often happen without you knowing it. So it's important to be able to identify them in order to better control them. It's no small task but, like with everything else, it's a skill you acquire through steely self-discipline and many hours of practice.

There are all sorts of tricks and habits you can use to avoid divulging information to your opponents. My first rule is to be quiet. I limit my chances of giving myself away by not saying anything. The things you say during a game may seem harmless, but they can tell a trained listener a lot. Your volume, tone and inflection, things you can't always control when you speak up spontaneously, can give you away.

Sure, some pros talk a lot at the table. They're not doing it to tell people how they're feeling — they talk to try to tease out information from their opponents. Daniel Negreanu is an expert in that art. You have to have a lot of talent and experience to be successful at it. And if you're not as good as he is, you should probably stay away from that tactic. Believe me: it's better to stay quiet. When you do have to talk — when you're passing, folding or placing your bet — it should be in the same manner, with the same expression and the same cold and indifferent tone throughout the whole game.

The other rule you should keep in mind is to come up with routine gestures, regardless of what's in your hand or what position you're in a game or tournament. That means developing a set of simple and coordinated mannerisms that will govern the way you place your hands on the table, how you hold your cards, the force with which you throw your chips down. You always have to act like you couldn't care less.

As you can see, a good poker player has to be a good actor. Since you know that your opponents are always trying to get a read on your game and your intentions, you may want send them down the wrong path by varying your attitude and your strategy. The ability to hide your emotions and cover your tracks is key to accumulating wins. It'll allow you to bet a modest amount on a hand your opponents think is okay, but which in reality is very good. They'll raise and bring up the value of the pot, which will win you a lot more money than if you'd bet big to start with and everyone else had folded. It'll also allow you to bluff on a hand that's so-so.

In short, any player who can control and hide his emotions and project indifference has a formidable weapon he can use whenever circumstances permit. But getting there requires a lot more training than you think. The key, as with most other facets of the game, is discipline.

6

Discipline

"To master poker and make it profitable, you must first master patience and discipline as lack of either is a sure disaster regardless of all other talents or lucky streaks." — **Freddie Gasperian**

Many experts say that discipline is a fundamental part of success in poker. I agree completely. You can't win regularly without meticulousness, consistency and a strong character. In fact, those qualities are the keys to success in all areas of life. Talent is meaningless when it's not supported by rigorous self-discipline.

Discipline refers to several aspects of a player's behavior both in and out of the game. I'm going to discuss three that strike me as particularly important: the importance of sticking with your plan when you're at the table; managing your bankroll (the money you have to spend on playing poker and registering in tournaments); and general lifestyle choices you have to make given that, at least in theory, being a poker player means having total freedom.

♠

Discipline first comes into play at the poker table. It's the one place where there's no room for improvisation, experience for the sake of experience or needless risk. You have to develop a sound strategy and stick to it regardless of the highs and lows you might experience along the way. Sure, your strategy is bound to shift based on who your opponents are and the size of your stack. What I mean by discipline here is the importance of remaining focused and in control of your game. And I want to stress again that poker is a methodical game: it's important not to let yourself get distracted by the temptation of easy money or a big win, or by the desire to make a quick comeback after you've lost a big hand.

The disciplined player's motto is simple: what helped me win regularly in the past will do so in the future. I say that because in high-stakes games and tournaments like the World Series, where there is no tomorrow, it can be tempting to modify your strategy when things aren't going your way. You can get away with it once in a while, especially if you're switching things up to confuse an opponent, but it should always be for the right reasons. Having discipline at the poker table means having confidence in your skills and in your system, and knowing that your profits will be smaller if you start going off in all directions.

It's easy to be disciplined when things are going well. It's when you're on tilt and your confidence is shaken that discipline is most important and most difficult to maintain.

In that type of situation, discipline doesn't only involve pot odds calculations, it also relates to playing within your means and properly managing your stack. You have to set strict rules and avoid deviating from them.

When I sat down at the final table during the 2010 WSOP, I was the chip leader. I was in a very comfortable position that gave me a significant advantage both mathematically and psychologically. I had a lot of leeway. I was in a position where I could take more risks if I had a good hand without having to worry about losing a good part of my stack. I also knew that my opponents — especially those with the fewest chips — wouldn't dare launch a frontal attack for fear of getting booted out of the tournament immediately.

However, the tables can turn so quickly. You have to stay disciplined even when you're in the lead. I speak from experience: from the moment play started at the final table, I experienced losses that saw my stack shrink by half. Which is all to say that even though you can play more aggressively when you're in the lead, you still can't allow yourself to waste your chips. You have to resist, at all costs, what I like to call the "temptation of the knock-out" — trying to quickly get rid of the players with the fewest chips. Sure, they're easy targets, and if an opportunity to eliminate them comes up, you should take it. But don't forget that they're in a place where they have nothing to lose. The strategy I adopted in that situation at the 2010 WSOP, which I'd use again, was to be cautious. When you're in the lead, it's better to let the players below you eliminate each other than risk losing chips when your hand doesn't warrant it.

When you're playing a cash game and you can leave the table whenever you want, you have to be disciplined not only in how you manage your stack but also in how you choose your opponents. This is especially true when you're playing online and can choose between hundreds of tables. If you realize that your opponents are much more skilled than you, don't hesitate to choose another table, even if the stakes are lower. The old adage "when there is no peril in the fight, there is no glory in the triumph" has absolutely no place in a poker game. No moral consideration should keep you from playing against — and beating — a player who is less talented than you. Have a field day — that's what those players are there for!

♠

Bankroll management also requires a lot of self-discipline. Most people who invest in poker — especially the beginners — aren't made of money, and have to keep track of the funds they put into it.

The first rule of thumb is never mix the money you need to live with the money you spend on poker. Those two categories have to be kept separate. Otherwise you risk playing and living beyond your means. And unless you're really lucky, you risk being unpleasantly surprised.

When managing your bankroll, you have to consider the natural variations in the game and try to minimize the impact of luck on your long-term results. In other words, you can't win every game, so you should never invest your entire bankroll in a single game or tournament. For example, if you have a $1,000 bankroll, you shouldn't sign up for a tournament with a $1,000 buy-in, or a $500 buy-in. The general rule is to avoid investing more than a certain percentage of your poker capital in a single tournament. For cautious players, that's usually 2% or 3%. More aggressive players go up to 5%. So, if you're an aggressive player, the maximum buy-in amount you should pay to play in a single tournament is $50. If you don't win anything, you'll still have enough money to ensure you can continue to play, which you need to do in order to keep moving up and improving your game. Because in poker, just like in other areas, it's practice that will make you a better player.

The same rule applies to cash games. If you have a $1,000 bankroll, you shouldn't play games where the blinds are more than 25¢/50¢. In this case, 25¢ is the small blind — the forced bet made by the player to the left of the dealer — and 50¢ is the big blind. The big blind is usually double the small blind; it's the amount players have to match in order to stay in the game to see the flop in a situation where no one raises. As a rule, you should always have 20 buy-ins. And your buy-in amount should equal the value of 100 big blinds. Ideally, especially when you start playing medium fixed-limit games, you should even have a minimum of 40 or 50 buy-ins. So let's come back to my earlier example: if you have $1,000 and you want to play 20 buy-ins, that means the maximum you can invest in the table is $50, which is equivalent to the buy-in at a table with 25¢/50¢ blinds. So you play that limit until you grow your bankroll to $2,000, or twenty 50¢/$1.00 buy-ins, and then you move to that next level.

Playing for such small stakes requires a lot of discipline for most players, because it seems like the profits will be very small. But that's not always the case. Pots can grow quickly, as can losses. That's why it's so important to establish limits.

If a player's bankroll shrinks as a result of repeated losses, he should be disciplined enough to reduce the stakes he's playing for. Unfortunately, many players, newer players especially, do exactly the opposite, raising the stakes in the hopes that they'll recover more quickly. The result? They put their bankroll at risk, and they often lose. And what happens then? They build a new bankroll from funds that weren't meant for poker. By doing that, they break the rule that poker funds must always be separate from other funds. And they forget that their previous bankroll needs to be added to the losses column. In the end, they create the illusion that they're better players than they actually are.

That said, these rules aren't immutable. You can choose to be more cautious or more aggressive, so long as you respect the basic guiding principles of bankroll management.

I'll admit that I haven't always followed the rules I'm laying out. If I had, I never would have signed up for the 2010 WSOP tournament, given that my bankroll would've had to total $200,000 for me to be able to afford the $10,000 buy-in — which it obviously didn't. In this case, like the hundreds of other players who registered for the tournament, I broke the rule for some very specific reasons, including the prestige of the tournament, the possible winnings and the possibility of earning an astronomical return on investment.

Why is discipline so hard to maintain, both when it comes to table play and bankroll management? Simply put, because it goes against the risk-taking nature of most of the people who gravitate towards games of chance. They're well aware of the necessity for strict discipline, but some find it very difficult to abide by it, while others simply aren't interested in playing by those rules. But know that those people will have very short careers. Some may argue that players like Phil Hellmuth, Jamie Gold and Allen Cunningham, who have all won millions of dollars playing tournaments, are rich enough now that they don't have to worry too much about their bankroll. That may be true, but one of the reasons they're at the top of the poker hierarchy today is because they once showed great discipline.

♠

You can't be disciplined in poker if you're not disciplined in life. That fact is even more true when you consider that people who choose to make poker their livelihood enjoy almost total freedom and aren't accountable to anyone: no boss, no clients, no board. They set their own hours, their eating habits and the number of hours they dedicate to the game.

You can compare a poker player to an entrepreneur who starts up his own business. However, unlike the entrepreneur who has employees to manage, the poker player takes all the responsibility on himself. Add to that the fact that poker players who turn pro are often young, and it becomes easy to understand why discipline is necessary to ensure stable and consistent play.

The pro player's main challenge is to treat poker like any other job. It's not always easy. You have to establish benchmarks, place limits and make choices that would be dictated by others or would only be necessary at more advanced levels in more traditional occupations. In other words, you have to be your own boss. It requires a high degree of motivation and an unwavering desire to attain very precise goals.

When you have a job and poker is only a hobby, you don't depend on it to put food on the table, even if you're making a lot of money at it. When you choose to make poker your main source of income, you're choosing to live without a safety net. From that moment on, your life depends on your performance. It's enormous additional pressure that casual players don't have to deal with. Prolonged downswings become more dangerous, and it can be more difficult to find your way out of them.

Even the most exciting activities can lose their appeal when they become the way you earn your living. Ask any athlete or professional artist. Once you're at that level, you have a new responsibility to perform regularly, both to put food on the table and to maintain your status in an elite group.

The other argument for maintaining strict self-discipline is the abundance of diversions that can distract poker players from their main focus. First-class trips, fancy hotels, discovering great cities and the glitz of Las Vegas and Atlantic City don't foster discipline. There's also the money, which attracts all kinds of people and activities of varying advisability. Conditions have improved in the past decades, but poker players still don't live in the most wholesome environment. They may no longer have Colts in their belts, but poker is still a world in which it's easy to give into temptation.

I've been very aware of those risks since I entered this world. That's why I do my best to maintain a healthy lifestyle. I try to maintain regular sleeping patterns, I watch what I eat, I exercise regularly and I avoid excesses. My reasons are simple: poker is my life, and my goal is to consistently place among the top players. So I direct all my energy to achieving that goal, and I systematically avoid anything that can put me off track.

A poker player's discipline is closely linked to his need to continue to improve his game by practicing, training, studying and analyzing past matches and great games played by others pros. I devote a good part of my day to it. In that way, I'm a lot like athletes and musicians who need to train every day both to avoid losing their edge and to maintain a high level of performance. In any field, excellence can be attributed in part to a strict discipline that stems from a desire to maintain one's place among the elite and to the perseverance that's needed to get there.

On Day 4 of the Main Event of the 2010 World Series, just as the money bubble is about to burst, I have Phil Galfond on my left, the best position from which to put the most pressure on me. The term "money bubble" refers to the point in the tournament at which the next player out will not win any money, while the rest of the players will. Many people consider Phil to be one of the best and most aggressive poker players around. While most of the other players were playing more cautiously to guarantee themselves a payday, Phil obviously wanted to force the bubble to burst. He was a constant threat.

I owed it to myself to play fewer hands and to be patient and disciplined. In a position like that, the best I could do was try to get to the end of day without too many losses and hope for a better table the next day — which wouldn't be too hard.

So I'm keeping my hand selection tight, only playing very strong starting hands. I raise with AS-QH in middle position. Galfond re-raises — no surprise — and a large sum at that. The action is back on me. We both have fairly big stacks. I don't call, because I can't play a pot against Galfond while out of position. So I have two choices: I can raise, or I can fold. The size of the stacks means that if I raise, it'll have to be an excessive amount, which is too risky for me so close to the payday zone. So, even though

I have a strong hand and an excellent chance of winning, I reluctantly fold.

When I thought about that move again after my head cleared, I decided that I should have been even more disciplined and folded before the flop. It might seem strange, but I think it's what the circumstances called for.

7

Perseverance

"If it were easy, everyone would do it."

— **Bonnie Damiano**

The legends of most great poker players were built on the cornerstone of an iron will and unfailing perseverance.

Daniel Negreanu went through a long dry spell before winning his first World Series bracelet in 1998 at the age of 23. His first Vegas experience had ended in spectacular failure two years prior, almost ruining him. His $3,000 bankroll hadn't even lasted two days. He went back to Vegas a few months later, having built himself a new bankroll, only to be cleaned out again. But he didn't give up. He knew his game wasn't good enough for the big leagues, so he went back to his hometown of Toronto to study strategy, perfect his game and play, play, play.

Finally, he had a breakthrough, and now he's considered one of the world's best players.

Scotty Nguyen came to the U.S. in 1974 at the age of 14, started playing poker at 16 and ended up so broke on his first trip to Vegas that he had to work as a croupier to rebuild his bankroll. He lost his bankroll several more times before he was able to register for the World Series in 1995, and he won the Main Event there three years later. Today, he's one of the top ten highest earners of all time.

The list of players who've lost small fortunes before finding their way to the top is very long.

I've been lucky to avoid burn-outs as spectacular as the ones I've described, but I've still been through some tough times and periods of great doubt in my quest for excellence. Downswings are inevitable, and it's easy to become discouraged when they happen. But they showed me, just like they've showed many others, that I still had a lot to learn. They put my determination to the test and challenged me to stay focused on my goal to become the best player I can be.

Even when you've reached the highest peak in the poker universe, there are things to remind you that no one is safe from going through a slump. Even the pros only have big paydays in a very small number of the tournaments they play. The size of the prize makes up for the registration fees they lose in tournaments from which they return empty-handed. Though they tend to win more often than they lose when they're playing cash games, it doesn't change the fact that the path of a pro player is strewn with situations where he's forced to demonstrate strength of character.

You're not born a professional poker player. You become one through talent, willpower, hard work and relentless perseverance.

Some people think the poker world is a glamorous place where a gang of golden boys who've had easy lives swim around in piles of money. But reality is much different than what you see on TV. Like me, the vast majority of top-ranked players come from poor or middle-class families. Several have at one time been poor or destitute. They're ordinary people who discovered their passion, patiently cultivated their talent and, through hard work and study, rose up through the ranks. Truthfully, things can't happen any other way when you're aiming for the top.

We're all born with certain talents. But, like Georges Brassens used to sing well before I was born, *without skill, a gift is nothing but a dirty habit.* He could've also added that without hard work, skill also has its limits.

I know some very good golf players who consistently maintain a five or six handicap — an excellent level that I will never reach — but who have never read a book on golf technique and who think practicing at a driving range is boring. Because of that, they know that in spite of their undeniable talent, they'll never make it to the major leagues. The same goes for poker: if you're not prepared to devote thousands of hours to studying, analyzing and playing the game, you may get to be a good player, but you'll never be a great one. There's nothing wrong with that — lots of people are fine with it — but that's the difference between putting in a good performance and excellence.

People have written thousands of books over the years that promise to divulge the secret to success. How to make friends. How to become rich and prosper. How to be happy in love. How to succeed in business. Each of those books contains a few basic truisms, techniques, methods and attitudes. But in the end it all adds up to only one thing: perseverance. What's perseverance? It's accepting that to become the master of any art you have to devote yourself to it entirely, and invest countless hours in it. Sometimes that's not even enough. All that work has to build on a basic amount of talent, passion and technical ability. It's not easy, but there's no other way.

In his bestselling book *Outliers: The Story of Success*, Canadian journalist Malcolm Gladwell writes that while pure genius doesn't exist, practice *can* make perfect. In other words, if you put in the time, you can become a great lawyer, a musical virtuoso . . . or a poker champion. Citing the research of several experts, Gladwell posits that it takes around 10,000 hours to properly master an art. It's a huge number when you think about it. It means that if you spend eight hours every day studying and playing poker, it will take you three and a half years to become a winner. If, like most people, you have a job and can only spend about three hours a day on poker, it'll take you nine years.

This supports the findings of a study conducted by Pokerftp .com, which analyzed more than a million hands played in cash games online. The data compiled by Pokerftp revealed that fewer than 20% of online players make a profit. However, 53% of people who've played more than 100,000 hands win money.

These results further support the indisputable fact that regardless of how talented you are, unless you complete a rigorous apprenticeship and put in considerable efforts and long hours of practice, you'll never be a dominant player.

> **ACCORDING TO JONATHAN:** "For me, perseverance is a constant refusal to fail. There can be no final defeat if you're still trying. No one accomplishes the extraordinary without extraordinary perseverance."

As I mentioned in an earlier chapter, I was smitten with poker from the first hand I ever played. I immediately wanted to know all of the game's secrets. One thing led to another and as I got better, just improving was no longer enough: I literally had to go through every step to become the best player I could be, and I was prepared to do anything to get there.

My generation grew up with the internet, so, naturally, it was the first place I looked for information. I quickly found several interesting paths there. My approach wasn't very systematic in the beginning. I was mostly exploring, and accumulating knowledge along the way, but I quickly realized that I needed to become familiar with general poker theory. I spent many hours reading up on poker strategy before I started playing regularly and testing out my knowledge in practice. I completed that basic training with the help of two authors who remain gurus to me to this day.

The textbook that taught me basic poker strategy is *The Theory of Poker: A Professional Poker Player Teaches You How to Think Like One* by David Sklansky, an expert who has written more than a dozen books on poker and who is a pro player in his own right, with three WSOP bracelets to his name. (Each player who wins a tournament in the World Series of Poker gets a WSOP bracelet. About 60 are awarded each year.) Considered by many to be the poker bible, you'll find this book on every serious poker player's bookshelf; I still consider it an essential read for anyone who wants to make their way up the poker ladder. Armed with countless examples, Sklansky addresses in a clear and simple fashion each and every question that matters when it comes to poker strategy, from pot odds to the importance of position to bluffing and psychology. Most importantly, he stresses how important it is to adapt your game to that of your opponents and to maximize the potential of your winning hands.

I've also learned a lot from three of Sklansky's other books: *Small Stakes Hold'em: Winning Big with Expert Play*, *Hold'em Poker for Advanced Players* and *No Limit Hold'em: Theory and Practice*. These books are more advanced, but still very clear. They'll help you with your study of strategy.

The other author who helped me concretize my knowledge of poker is Dan Harrington, a remarkable player who won the Main Event of the 1995 World Series of Poker who is also a champion backgammon and chess player. His trilogy, *Harrington on Hold'em: Expert Strategy for No-Limit Tournaments*, is focused exclusively on no-limit tournament play. In its 1,400 pages, you'll learn about basic tournament strategy, starting hand selection and advanced concepts of play. The third volume of the trilogy is particularly interesting, as it offers an illustrated analysis of 50 situations experienced in World Series tournaments by some of the world's best players, including Phil Ivey, Phil Hellmuth, Daniel Negreanu and Mike Matusow. In my opinion, this trilogy is indispensable for anyone wishing to improve at poker.

Having completed my study of theory, I moved on to play, which is far from the best way to guarantee improvement. However, I never thought at that time that I was ready to face elite players. I was still testing out the theories I'd studied up until that point, and I was very conscious of the fact that I still had a lot to learn. I knew that I'd make lots of amateur mistakes, and that I'd have to learn from them. That's how you get better.

Of course, when you've taken in so much theoretical knowledge, you start to feel as though you suddenly understand tons of things you never knew existed, and you start to feel like you've made huge inroads. Lots of people start feeling powerful and even invincible at this point. But reality quickly brings them back to earth. If you really want to get better at something, the key is to remain modest and clear-headed while keeping your self-confidence intact.

No matter where you are on the poker ladder, you should never let yourself believe that you've reached the top and that you have nothing more to learn and no longer need to make an effort. From the start, I was very conscious of how important analyzing my performance would be to cementing my knowledge and continuing to improve. I've never stopped doing that. I analyze every hand I play, whether it's played online or in a tournament, and I pay special attention to the high stakes hands.

It's important to be both discerning and objective when

you're running that kind of analysis, because it's very easy, especially when you're starting out, to make up stories. You have to remember that just because you won a hand doesn't mean it was well played. The opposite is also true.

If you're playing online, there are several programs you can buy that make this kind of analysis a lot easier. Software packages like Hold'em Manager and Poker Tracker collect data from every hand you've played and generate stats and important information on your habits, and in which positions and situations you've won or lost the most money. They also collect indispensable information on your opponents: who is aggressive and who is more cautious, who bets most often before the flop, which hands have the most action based on the number of players at the table, and so on. Any serious player who wants to improve his game should take advantage of these kinds of tools.

The rise of the internet has had a hugely positive effect on the game of poker worldwide. Not only has it democratized the game, online poker has also led to a significant increase in the number of good players around the world. Before, a person who wanted to play had to travel to where his opponents were, which wasn't always easy for people who live far from urban centers. Today, all it takes is a computer with an internet connection and voilà, you can play as many games as you want with as many players as you want and for the stakes that you've chosen. You can even play for free using virtual money, which allows you to quickly improve your game and at little expense. You can start betting when you feel ready and move on to the higher levels as you improve. That's what I did.

That said, it takes a certain amount of clear-headedness to know when you're ready to move on to the next step. And that quality also plays a role in perseverance. Even if he's extremely motivated to become a better player, the determined player will continue to play at lower levels because he's methodical and patient in his desire to improve. He refuses to skip any steps.

♥

It's reassuring to think if you put in the time and the effort, you're guaranteed to become a poker champion. But don't kid yourself: that's not always how it happens. Think of all the young baseball and hockey players who'll do just about anything to make it to the majors, but who never make it past the minors. Hard work is crucial, but for most people, it's not enough. Not everyone can be Wayne Gretzky or Babe Ruth.

In poker, like in other fields, there's often a moment when you reach your top limit and you start to level off. This phenomenon was identified decades ago as the Peter Principle, which states that "in a hierarchy every employee tends to rise to his level of incompetence." In other words, you will inevitably reach a level that you can't exceed. To start winning again, you have to go back to a lower level.

That's when many players start moving back and forth between two levels, becoming a bit like the journeymen of pro sports who spend their careers going between the major and minor leagues. Many of them either get discouraged, or they end up coming to terms with their fate and become satisfied with the level where they win. Others, and these players are more rare, persist and succeed in making it to the highest poker circles.

This is all to say that while determination and perseverance are necessary to get to the top, they're not necessarily going to solve all your problems. When it comes to poker, some skills are easier to master than others. One of them includes being able to read your opponents.

8

Psychology

"You have to learn what kind of hand this guy shows down, what that one's moves are, watch the veins in his neck, watch his eyes, the way he sweats."

— **Johnny Moss**

Even though I've used him as an example several times already in this book — mainly because he's one of the world's best players and I greatly admire him — it's hard for me not to start this chapter on psychology without again mentioning master reader Daniel Negreanu.

Daniel is a rare bird: an unrepentant and congenial chatterbox who is extremely kind and loved by everyone at the table. However, beneath his friendly exterior lurks a formidable predator who, by his own admission, uses his innate talent as a communicator to glean the most information he can from his opponents in order to use it to his advantage during a game or tournament. The more another player divulges about himself, whether verbally or through his body language, the better Negreanu can evaluate his personality, his state of mind and the way he plays. Negreanu is remarkably good at psychologically profiling his opponents and, based on a player's decisions and behavior, at guessing what cards he has in his hand. What's most impressive is that, though he talks a lot at the table, he's one of the most difficult players to read.

♦

If the most important poker skill were being able to calculate pot odds, it would be a fairly easy game. All you'd need to regularly win hands is math expertise. What makes poker such a complex and fascinating game is the human element, the mental strategy that comes into play and often makes the difference between a win and a loss. This is especially true when you're playing at a level where the players are more or less of equal strength.

The players who are the best at reading their opponents have a significant advantage because they're better able to figure out not only what's in their opponents' hands, but how aggressively they're playing, how likely they are to bluff or how confident they are. Armed with that information, a player is able to make better decisions.

I'm often asked to define my playing style. Am I aggressive, conservative, daring, cautious? I invariably respond that I don't have a style, that my opponents' style is my style. People may think it's a joke but it's not. That's really how I think and play. I have to adapt my style to the players I face. Because if they're able to adapt to the way I play — in other words, if they're able to understand the motivations behind each of my plays — I may as well leave the table. I'm done.

When I'm sitting at a poker table — especially one where I'm joined by players I know very little or not at all — I know that to win, I have to quickly figure out who I'm dealing with.

Every player is a new door I have to unlock. I want to get inside their brain and hear their thoughts, so I can figure out their next steps. I want to know the strength of each player's hand, what they're feeling during key strategic moments and, of course, the plays they're going to make. I especially want to know why a certain player behaves in a certain way. I should never assume that their motivations are the same as mine. The logic behind this strategy is simple: the more I know about my opponents, the more likely I will be able to control the game.

In poker terminology, everything that relates to psychology — everything that doesn't specifically have to do with card distribution and probability calculations — is known as the "meta-game." The meta-game is the game-within-the-game that I've frequently referred to in this book. The meta-game refers to match-up histories, to how I perceive other players and how they perceive me, to the clues we uncover about each other's games. It's everything that's unquantifiable in a poker competition.

Once you're at this level, you're not just playing poker anymore — you're engaged in a battle of wills.

♦

The first thing you have to consider when you're trying to read your opponents is how they bet. Each player has different protocols for different situations, and most players have a tendency to react the same way when faced with the same hand. Some players bet big when they have a good hand, so they can protect their profit possibilities and force other players to fold. Others will bet small in the hopes that their opponent will call, thus increasing the size of the pot. (Lots of beginners use this strategy to try to raise the stakes, but it's not the most efficient method; the best way to increase the value of a pot is to place big bets.) Other players bluff on weak or medium hands. In each of these situations, I have to identify each player's style and his motivations for acting the way he does.

After studying my opponents' bets for several hands, things start to make sense: a kind of labyrinth appears in my brain and, by traveling through it, I'm able to uncover each player's habits. Those habits tell me more about a player's way of thinking — whether they're timid, cautious or aggressive — as well as about the range of hands that are likely to correspond to the number of chips they're betting. For example, if a player bets 50 chips before the flop, I'll know he has a medium pair. If he bets 100 chips, he has a high pair or A-K or A-Q. If he bets 100 chips on the turn, I have to assume he's looking to draw a straight, a flush or trips. This will help me guess how he'll react to a raise, as well as how often he's likely to bluff. By being able to guess how he'll react, I have a net advantage over him, like a chess player who can see several moves ahead.

The best poker players are able to use psychology to their advantage, to get into their opponents' heads. I'm very proud — and I say this with all due modesty — to have perfected my ability to read my opponents over the years, and to understand their ways of thinking and to interpret their table behavior. It's become second nature for me, and it played a huge role in my 2010 WSOP win.

Of course, my attempts to get into my opponents' heads don't always work. They know I'm trying to get a read on their betting habits, and they're trying to do the same with me. That's why players try to make themselves seem unpredictable by betting differently from time to time, to switch things up and lead me astray. Some will bet small when they have a strong hand. Others will bet big with a weak hand, even if it means they might lose their bet. As every high-level player knows, it's worth losing a small bet if you can cast uncertainty in your opponents' minds and win a big pot down the road.

My ability to get inside my opponents' heads was put to the test at the final table of the Main Event of the 2010 WSOP. One of the players I found most difficult to read was Joseph Cheong, a rising star on the poker circuit who placed third overall in the tournament.

Cheong played very aggressively, continually modifying his betting habits and putting a lot of pressure on his opponents by keeping them guessing. In the end though, he did himself in, losing 176.4 million chips — the biggest pot in poker history — on a hand that paved the way for me to win the tournament.

Cheong had AS-7H to my QC-QD after six-bet shoving all-in before the flop. I called. The flop came 3D-9H-2C, and Cheong was desperate for the ace that would win him the hand and pretty much eliminate me from the tournament. 6S came out on the turn. Cheong only had three outs left on the river, which came down 8S. My pocket queens held. Joseph Cheong had fewer than 10 million chips, which meant that his elimination was just a formality. And I ended up with around 85% of the chips, which made me the favorite going into the final heads-up against John Racener.

I think the meta-game played a critical role in that hand. Some say Cheong fished too aggressively by going all-in, but I don't agree with that analysis. His A-7 hand was strong enough for a three-player table. He just had some bad luck. Moreover, in the past few hands at the final table, we'd often re-raised, and I'd almost always folded after the four-bet. He probably thought I'd do that again. When I five-bet, he had good reasons to think that I was trying to adjust to his frequent re-raises by adding another level of aggressiveness. By going all-in, he responded to how he perceived I was adjusting to his aggressive tactics, likely never thinking that I'd call. As for me, I also had a strong hand for a three-player table, and I knew that Cheong had been on the offensive the whole time we were at the final table and that the strength of his hand probably didn't warrant the size of his bets. That example brings me to another important part of the meta-game: getting to know different levels of thought.

♦

To win regularly at poker, you need to be able to do more than just figure out betting habits, styles of play, levels of aggressiveness and strategy. You also need to be able to perform increasingly complex levels of analysis.

The first level of thought in a game is about your own hand, and it ignores any other considerations relating to your opponents. You base your play on the cards you've been dealt. That's usually how beginners and casual players play.

In the second level, you start to analyze your opponents' game, their table behavior, and how often and how much they bet. Players who are at this level are a bit more advanced, but they don't usually win with any regularity.

The third level is more complicated: it involves using the information you have on hand to put yourself in your opponent's shoes and guess what he's thinking of your game. Does he think I have a strong hand? That I'm hoping to complete a straight or a flush? That I'm bluffing? That I will or won't call a big re-raise? If you can get to this level, you'll be a winner.

When you reach the fourth level, you're faced with this question: What does my opponent think I think he has in his hand? Too complicated? Maybe, but you can't be part of the poker elite without asking yourself that kind of question. Once you've mastered that mental cat-and-mouse game, you'll be able to call bluffs, limit your losses on weaker hands and maximize your profit possibilities on strong ones.

When two players who know each other well go heads-up, things can get even more complicated. If you happen to catch that kind of match-up during a televised tournament, you might find some of the decisions a bit unusual. But rest assured: these players know what they're doing. For example, in the hand with Joseph Cheong, we were way deeper than the fourth level — probably nearing the eighth or the ninth. That's why his decision to go all-in with an A-7 — a medium hand that still had some potential in a heads-up situation — wasn't really as surprising as you might think.

In spite of all this, you're wrong if you think that high-level thinkers should deploy their full psychological arsenal against weaker players. As they say, it takes two to tango. If you're on level four and your opponent is on level one, it won't do you any good to go further in your analysis, because your opponent is only focused on his own hand, nothing else. It'd be like wasting all your energy fighting your shadow. People generally agree that to have the best chances to win, you should think one level ahead of your opponent. If you're playing a level-two player, you should play no higher than level three. If you think at a higher level, you'll start to play as though your opponent is a better player than he actually is. You'll set traps that are too elaborate, he won't fall for them and you'll be the one who suffers in the end.

♦

Don't think of the psychology of poker as a battle of egos. Thinking that way puts you at risk of being ruled by emotion, which is likely to reduce your ability to think clearly and make good decisions. You should never succumb to the temptation of making poker confrontations personal. The minute you do, you'll stop thinking long term. For example, you should never let your pride get in the way of losing small pots, because you may win a bigger one down the road. The goal in poker isn't to win hands; it's to win chips and money. I don't mind losing nine out of 10 hands, if the hand I do win earns me more than what I've lost. That's the logic that has to prevail at the table.

The other mistake you should never make when you're trying to get into someone's head and figure out their motivations is to assume that they think the same way you do. Every player is unique. Identical situations will result in different strategies from different players. Players choose different ways of achieving the same goal. Some bluff more than others, bet bigger or fold more easily. Some play offense, others defense. The range of possible personalities, behaviors and strategies requires that you move beyond any preconceived notions you may have and think long and hard when you're making a decision. Otherwise you risk making mistakes about the true nature of your opponents and paying for it.

In closing, don't forget that you should know yourself as well if not better than you know your opponents. If you don't, you might end up becoming your own worst enemy.

9

Knowing Yourself

"The single greatest key to winning is knowing thy

enemy: yourself." — **Andy Glazer**

If you can't stand the sight of blood, you probably shouldn't become a doctor. If you don't like numbers, you likely wouldn't consider becoming an accountant. If you're afraid of flying, you should think twice before getting your pilot's license. Same goes for poker: if you're no good under pressure, if you give in to every impulse or if the idea of losing a dollar gives you hives, you'll never win consistently at poker. You have to know yourself well before you decide what you're going to do with your life.

Poker psychology involves more than just being able to figure out your opponents' intentions. It pertains first and foremost to knowing yourself. And that requires an unwavering clear-headedness, free of complacency and self-delusion, before, after and especially during a match. If you think knowing your opponents will help you win at poker, you're absolutely right. But you'd be wrong to think that has little to do with you.

When you commit to poker and start investing large amounts of money and time in the game, you have to be straight with yourself. You can't think you're a better or worse player than you actually are. You have to know where you stand, what your strengths and your weaknesses are and how to build a foundation using the former while doing everything in your power to minimize the effects of the latter. You also have to know how to avoid situations where your opponents will have the opportunity to take advantage of your weaknesses.

Perfect poker players don't exist. No player is invincible. There's no poker equivalent of Roger Federer or Tiger Woods — no player sits at the top of the heap for years. Luck makes it impossible for any one player to dominate in a consistent way. Even the best players can be beaten. That's why it's so important to be able to take maximum advantage of the elements of the game that you can control.

In poker, as in other sports, every player has his strengths. Joe Hachem's is self-discipline. Phil Ivey is known for his level of concentration and his self-control. Gus Hansen is really good at calculating implied pot odds. Phil Hellmuth's desire to win is almost unmatched and is most obvious in his arrogance and unsavory character.

Even though I have less experience than the veteran players I just named, I feel like I have a fairly good handle on what kind of player I am. One of my greatest strengths is my ability to control my emotions no matter what kind of pressure I'm under. My math skills are good, and I manage my bankroll well. I think I'm fairly good at quickly reading my opponents' betting habits but, like many players who came up playing online poker, I'm not as good at reading their behaviors or their tells. My weaknesses include excessively aggressive play at tables with up to nine or 10 players. That's because I like to be part of the action. Since it takes longer to play a nine- or 10-person hand, I have a tendency to become impatient and bet more often than I should. In those kinds of hands, I tend to bluff 18% to 20% of the time; that percentage should be closer to 15%. It's a risky way to play, given that the more players there are at a table, the greater chance there is that one of them will have a strong hand.

I don't know a single player who doesn't have weaknesses or limitations. Some don't play as well when they're hungry. Others have a harder time picking themselves up after they lose a big hand. And others find their concentration fails them after a few hours of play.

Every elite player knows his strengths as well as he knows his weaknesses, and he's always aware of them when he's at the table. If you know you're vulnerable when you're hungry, eat small snacks as regularly as you can in order to avoid having your digestion affect your play. If you become disappointed and unsure of yourself after you lose a big pot, take a break for a few hands. And if your concentration dulls after a few hours, you might want to focus on cash games, where you can leave the table at any time, instead of tournaments.

You lose because of your mistakes, and that can be a scary thought. When you think about it more carefully though, you realize that many of those mistakes — especially when it comes to experienced players — are caused by lapses in concentration or by an inability to control one's emotions, which is almost always caused by exhaustion or sometimes even boredom.

I've said it before: poker is a mental sport, a game of intellect that requires intense and sustained analysis that can be extremely exhausting in the long run. That's why you should never play when you're tired. In poker, as in any sport or intellectual pursuit, you're more likely to make mistakes when you're feeling tired. Of course, when I'm in tournament mode, I have to play even if I'm not at my best. All the more reason to make sure that my body and my mind can withstand the wear and tear that's caused by a long poker session. You have to have a healthy lifestyle (this is something I'll come back to in a later chapter), leave your personal problems at home and try to relax, so you never lose that desire to play. When poker becomes your job, it can be easy to forget that playing should always be enjoyable, a challenge you've accepted that's made more interesting because of the risk involved. Losing your competitive edge can be like giving up the fight, the surest road to defeat.

♣

There's another aspect of knowing yourself that comes into play in poker. It involves being able to take a step back from yourself, away from your strengths and limitations. You need to have enough perspective to be able to evaluate your game as though it were someone else's. That means being both discerning and objective.

It's easy to fool yourself in poker. When you're winning, you tend to think it's because you're playing well; when you lose, you want to blame your losses on bad luck. It's only human. That's why it's so important to be able to be neutral — dispassionate, even — when you're sizing up your opponents, your own hand and the level at which the game is unfolding. Being able to be clear-eyed and objective in a game will help you control play and avoid becoming prey to your emotions.

In poker, the hand you have is not as important as the hand your opponents think you have. If you can fool them, you'll win more often, even if most of your hands are actually weak. A player who knows himself well can control play by projecting the image he wants and influencing how other players perceive him. In the end, it's all about turning your weaknesses into traps for your opponents.

If I know my strengths and my weaknesses and I can take a

few steps back from the situation and get an objective read on it, then I can use my weaknesses to my advantage. For example, let's say I tend to be a little shy about raising on the river. I think it's a bit ruthless and I almost never do it. My opponent will probably notice this, and he'll be tempted to be bolder at that stage of the game. But since I know he's figured out that tendency in my game, my chances of getting away with a bluff are higher because by raising on the river, I'm planting a doubt in his mind. He'll probably figure I have a strong hand and chances are that he won't try to go up against me.

This brings us back to the levels of thought I discussed in the last chapter. In addition to the questions I usually ask myself — What's my opponent's game? What does he think I have? What does he think I think he has? — there's an additional dimension, the one where my knowledge of myself allows me to create a version of myself for my opponents that can allow me to better control the game. My goal is to make them believe that they've understood a certain behavioral pattern and then to act in a contradictory manner. That's the cat-and-mouse-game: to constantly try to deceive and destabilize your opponents, to back them into a corner only to reappear somewhere else moments later. By being elusive, you drain your opponents' confidence and concentration, which can cause them to make mistakes. No wonder some people call poker the most dangerous game that's played sitting down.

Knowing yourself isn't limited to knowing your strengths and weaknesses. You also have to be able to integrate them and those of your opponents into an objective evaluation of the situation at hand. You have to be able to distance yourself from play and see it from above, like a general watching a battle from his perch on the ridge. He clearly sees the position of his troops as well as those of his enemy, and he's able to analyze the impact and importance of each movement and to make the necessary adjustments as the situation evolves.

But remember, you're not playing chess or backgammon. You can never have a completely clear read in poker, because you don't know what cards your opponent has. Poker is a game in which you have to make decisions based on incomplete information. But if you know your opponents well enough, know how aggressive or tight they are, know their betting habits, and you can control the image you project at the table, you have a fairly accurate picture of the situation, and you'll be able to make the most of the information you have. It won't work every time, but it'll pay off eventually.

"It is said that if you know your enemies and know yourself, you will not be imperiled in a hundred battles," wrote Sun Tzu in *The Art of War*. It's an aphorism that could be the epigraph to any book on the art of poker.

♣

There are many ways to become better acquainted with the kind of poker player you are. The first, and one that anybody hoping to improve at anything in life should make use of, is to analyze your behaviors and your mistakes and draw lessons from them. Coaches use video replays to show their players where their weaknesses are, and poker players who want to improve should take the time to analyze their matches. I spend at least an hour a day on it. As I mentioned in a previous chapter, if you're playing online, you can buy software that will keep track of your playing history and produce hand-by-hand analysis. It's an incredibly useful tool, especially for beginners and intermediate players who may have a hard time identifying their weaknesses.

Another way you can evaluate and improve your ability to adapt is to play a different variation of poker once in a while. If your specialty is Texas Hold'em, which is currently the most popular variant, try playing Omaha, seven-card stud or good old five-card draw. It'll give you a new perspective, give your game more flexibility, stimulate your creativity and add a few additional weapons to your arsenal of strategies. If you think you might make some real money at poker someday, it'll be a far more profitable endeavor if you know all of the game's variants. That way you won't be confined to only one variant during the World Series of Poker, for example, which will let you increase your profit possibilities.

It's also not a bad idea to play low-stakes or no-stakes games. It's easy to do online, and it's a good way to test out new strategies. You may end up in different types of situations than you're used to, and you can then analyze your behavior and see whether or not you succeed. It's another way of getting to know what kind of poker player you are, and what kind of player you could become.

Before the 2010 WSOP, I mostly played online and focused on cash games. I usually played on ten $2/$4 and $5/$10 no-limit PokerStars Hold'em tables at the same time.

On one particular day, I'd lost several hands in a short time, as often happens, but I wasn't too worried, and I actually felt like I was playing my best poker. Then along came this huge hand that made me think I might win back the day's losses in one go.

Both my opponent — a player I consider to be very weak — and I have deep stacks. I consider him to be a fish. I have pocket aces, so I can't hope for a better situation when he raises. I re-raise and I'm very happy when he does too. But he's not usually this aggressive. Could he really have a strong hand? Maybe, but probably not as strong as mine.

Given how deep our stacks are, I figure he won't be able to fold if I raise again. So I re-raise and, to my great surprise, so does he. I go all-in with a total of $4,000, or four buy-ins on a $5/$10 table. He calls and shows off suited

A-K. At that moment, I have a 93.47% chance of winning the hand, one of the best possible pre-flop leads.

10H-JS-QC on the flop gives him a straight. It's hard to imagine a worse situation. He goes from being an outsider to being a favorite with a 91.67% chance of winning the hand, which, in the end, is what ends up happening. Under normal circumstances, I would've stayed at the table in a situation like that in order to profit off a weak player with a lot of money.

I'm usually quite good at controlling my emotions. But that day I went on tilt, which could've meant big additional losses. Luckily, I was clear-headed enough to know my state of mind. My self-awareness urged me to leave the table, turn off the computer and do other things for the rest of the day. I'm convinced I would've lost more money if I'd continued to play in the state I was in. In a way, I would've become the fish.

10

The Thirst for Victory

"Very seldom do the lambs slaughter the butcher."

— Amarillo Slim

Since I won the Main Event of the WSOP in November 2010, people talk to me more about the $8.9 million I won than about the win itself. I know it's more money than most people will see in their lifetimes, but I'm still a bit perplexed when it comes to remarks about it. In my mind, the fact that I beat 7,300 players in the world's most prestigious poker tournament to become the champion is infinitely more impressive than any sum of money that came with the win.

Of course, I'm happy to have won such a huge sum of money, but to me the prize is payment for a lot of hard work and a testament to the fact that I beat the world's best players to win that year's tournament.

♠

You're dead wrong if you think financial gain is a pro poker player's main motivation. None of the top players I know on the American and European circuits got into poker to make money. In fact, most players who become involved in this very competitive environment solely to get rich usually end up becoming poorer. Poker isn't about accounting. Money is secondary, even if, paradoxically, we measure a poker player's success by how much he's won. The most important thing is to win, collect WSOP bracelets and be among the best.

Here too there's an analogy to be made between poker and pro sports. Pro players want to earn what the market thinks is fair, but I think most of them would willingly give up part of their salary to see their name on the Stanley Cup, the Commissioner's Trophy or the Claret Jug.

In poker, like in any other competition, you don't get far without a strong desire to win. It's what sets the great players apart from the others, and it's often what helps them win those crucial matches. Think of legendary athletes like Maurice Richard, Reggie Jackson or Tiger Woods, who could bring up their game a few notches in the playoffs or during important tournaments. It's the people who are motivated who rise above the rest. It's that thirst for victory that gives the best players that extra energy and concentration that makes all the difference.

How do you describe a thirst for victory? It's a state of mind that borders on obsession, one where your entire being strives towards one goal: victory. Not money, not accolades, not recognition — all that counts is winning. A player who's driven by a desire to win is in a state of war. The other players around the table are enemies to be destroyed. He fears nothing, no one; he has no pity. He's ready for anything. Let there be no mistake: the desire for victory is the height of egotism. It's the moment where Dr. Jekyll turns into Mr. Hyde.

Most players on the pro poker tour are nice, likable people with whom I have a good rapport. A lot of them work with charitable organizations on causes they really believe in. (I recently started working with One Drop in order to increase awareness about the importance of equitable access to clean water.) But when those players sit down at a World Series table, there's no room for charity. They turn into machines with only one goal: winning. You can tell them apart pretty easily: they're the ones who worry about their financial profit about as much as they do about the first cavity they ever had. The only thing they want is to win.

There comes a point in a tournament, usually about midway through, where every remaining player is guaranteed to win some money. That's called "being on the bubble." As that moment approaches, many players will play more tightly in the hopes of staying in the game long enough to win money. They'll play fewer hands, be less aggressive, bet less and think twice about re-raising on big bets. Those players aren't playing to win enough chips to make it to the final table: they just want to place so they can put money in their pockets. It's very rare that one of those players will win a tournament. The reason is simple: you have to take risks to win and make your dreams come true. You have to be prepared to lose it all in one hand if you think it's worth it. True winners don't hesitate to take those chances — even though the risks they take are always carefully calculated.

That said, and contrary to what many might think, you can't give your thirst for victory free reign. Quite the opposite. It's a state of mind that requires great self-control and unwavering concentration.

ACCORDING TO JONATHAN: "The desire to win is a quality that's shared by all winners, regardless of the field. You don't win unless every cell in your body fervently wants it."

In poker, like in other competitive situations, the thirst for victory manifests as constant aggressiveness, regardless of the circumstances. They say you shouldn't kick a man when he's down. Apologies to any sensitive souls out there, but that rule doesn't apply in poker. When your opponent is on his way out, you've got to finish him off so he doesn't get up and take all your chips on the next hand. I have to be ruthless, especially since I know that my opponents won't hold back either. It's every man for himself. It can't be any other way.

That killer instinct isn't easy to maintain, especially when you're winning a lot in a cash game. From playing games with friends, I've learned that it's easy to play like the good guy you are in your daily life when you're having a good night. You let your guard down a bit, you become less aggressive, you worry less about the size of your stack. It's as though a voice is telling you that you've won enough and you should give other people a chance. But unless you get a series of very good hands, this is always when you start to lose. When the flame starts to falter, it's time to leave the table.

While pro players don't often consciously display generosity towards their fellow players, they're still not safe from seeing their thirst for victory fade. At the start of a tournament, especially the Main Event of the World Series of Poker, you can be sure that most players are pumped. The desire to play and to win is intense. However, for varying reasons, most will see their obsession with winning fade as the competition progresses.

In pro sports, the desire to win is only maintained over a relatively short period. A hockey game usually lasts between two and a half and three hours (if you take into consideration stoppages of play and the two intermissions); a baseball game lasts about three hours; a golf game around four. A poker tournament, meanwhile, is spread over several 10-hour days. It's not easy to maintain your intensity over that length of time. Every player goes through high and low periods and has to fight to retain that desire to win.

The most common reason for a drop in intensity is fatigue, which is far and away the worst enemy of a poker player in a tournament. Fatigue dulls your senses, and especially your ability to concentrate and to control your emotions. You have to start prepping your body to withstand the long hours of effort well in advance of the tournament.

Tilt also affects the desire to win, that insidious emotion caused by a prolonged stretch of bad hands. The first thing that falls to tilt is self-confidence. And once you start doubting yourself, it's tough to maintain that thirst for victory that will propel you to the top. You're worn down, sometimes panic stricken; your judgment is off, and that affects your concentration. It becomes more difficult to be disciplined and make good decisions. What's more, some players — usually those who've already won the World Series or other high-profile tournaments — become blasé, as though winning one tournament is good enough, and there's nothing left to prove. They start playing like robots, displaying impeccable technique and using all the right tricks, but without that fire that you need to win.

When you feel that thirst for victory disappearing during a tournament, it's tough to get it back, especially given the time constraints. You see your chips start to disappear and your first instinct is to stop the hemorrhage. Being on the verge of elimination, like I was during the second round of the Main Event of the 2011 WSOP, affects your thirst for victory. You find yourself in a situation where victory is a faraway goal, at the end of a road filled with obstacles. You go into survival mode and have to proceed step by step. In those situations, you can lose control of your game, take crazy risks and put it all on the line, like a baseball team that's down by three in the bottom of the ninth with two outs and bases empty.

♠

It's one thing for a downswing or fatigue to affect your desire to win over the course of a tournament. It's another thing to become a kind of poker functionary, to altogether cease being driven by that thirst for victory.

It can be tough to maintain that motivation when poker is your primary income-generating occupation. The *need* to win money takes precedence over the *will* to win. Winning stops being the end goal, edged out by the need for a return on investment. For example, if a tournament has a buy-in of $5,000, you'll want to make that money back and then some before starting to think about the big win and its honors.

This is a pretty common occurrence. When poker becomes your livelihood, financial considerations come into play, which distract you from your original passion. Financial motivation becomes more important, and everything else becomes routine. And for some players, there's nothing wrong with that. Everyone makes their own choices in life. But the reality is that when the game becomes more technical and mechanical, profits fall. A player who's mainly motivated by money will subconsciously rely more on his technical abilities than his passion to win. He'll make less of an effort, and his interest for the game, his will to improve and his desire to win will drop. Playing will stop being pleasurable, and he'll lose his desire to reinvent himself, explore his creativity and find new ways to win.

You can't play your best if you don't feel that passion for victory and improvement, that beginner's excitement you felt when the stakes were almost non-existent.

You also have to remain unaffected by the amount of money in play up to a certain point, regardless of the size of the bets. Poker can be a difficult game without nerves of steel.

Nerves of Steel

"There is no real cash game without risk-taking. You have to put yourself in harm's way to win at high levels. You have to be ready to bleed. You have to have your back against the wall. Or else you'll never give it your all." — **Doyle Brunson**

When I sit down at a poker table, whether in a tournament or in a no-limit cash game, I know that my nerves are going to be put to the test. Check-raises, slow games, all-ins, wild re-raises — they all affect my emotions in circumstances where concentration, discipline, self-control and good judgment are indispensable.

I've said it before: in many ways, poker is a battle of wills. Everyone's trying to get under everyone else's skin; to make them crack; to cast doubt, confusion and fear in their minds — fear of losing, of looking like an idiot or like a coward who falls apart when things really get going, of not being able to read a bluff and, especially, of losing a huge amount of money or of being eliminated from a tournament.

If I have a low pair and a player bets 10% of the value of my stack, it's easy for me to call. I don't have a lot to lose. It's a whole other story if he bets the equivalent of 90% of my stack.

Every experienced player has been in situations that got his adrenaline pumping. Your opponent just went all-in and you have to decide whether to risk a huge amount of money, and maybe even your chance of survival in the tournament. Your pulse speeds up, your chest gets tight, you start to sweat but you have to keep things under control or else give yourself away. The different possible outcomes, good and bad, start crashing around in your mind. And the questions follow: What does he have in his hand? Is he bluffing? What cards do I need to win?

The more you move up in the poker world, the more risky situations you'll encounter. The higher the stakes, the higher the pots and the profits. If you can win big pots, you can also lose them. And you're probably not going to win big hands if you're not prepared to lose large sums of money. It's just basic logic. If you're not comfortable taking risks, you'll lose less money and fewer chips, but your profits won't be as big. That approach might work in cash games, but it'll never work in tournaments, where the players with the most chips can eliminate those with the fewest in a single hand. It's like the old poker maxim goes: you don't win a tournament by folding. The reality is that you can't win big without betting big . . . But every time you bet big, your nerves pay the price.

One of the most controversial hands of the Main Event of the 2010 WSOP, one that was crucial to my victory (you can watch this hand on YouTube at http://www.youtube.com/watch?v=PMHwtN_wD0Q) explains what I mean.

By this point in the tournament, there were only 15 players remaining over two tables. I was in second place in chips and Matt Affleck, a very talented young player with impressive stats, was third. After the pocket cards are dealt, I end up with JH-JC a great hand. Matt has even better: AS-AC. Of course, neither of us knew what the other person had. With two high pairs, we were in a situation where the bets were likely to be quite high, and where one player would probably lose most of his chips. And luck wasn't in my corner. Affleck's aces were favored to win at 81% before the community cards were dealt.

Confident in my pair of jacks and first to speak before the flop, I bet 575,000 chips. Affleck raised me 1,550,000. After the other players folded, I re-raised almost four million chips. Affleck called. 10D-9C-7H came out on the flop. At that point, even if I didn't think Affleck had a better hand than me, it still had to be a possibility given how aggressively he was playing. For that reason, I hoped the pot would stay small. But Affleck's pair of aces was favored to win at 73%, which, of course, I didn't know at the time.

Affleck bet five million chips after the flop, and I matched his bet, which pushed the pot to 18,450,000. Things were starting to get serious, and it was obvious that the chip rankings would be significantly different after the hand. QD came out on the turn, which gave me a straight draw and still a possibility for three of a kind. With my 9-10-J-Q open-ended straight possibility, an 8, J or K would give me a win. The whole time, I was convinced that Affleck didn't have as good a hand as he actually did. Two pair, maybe 10 and 9, but not a pair of aces.

That's when Affleck went all-in for 11.6 million chips. If he won the hand, he'd be the new chip leader with a huge advantage. If he lost, he'd go home to Seattle with about $500,000.

I had a very difficult decision to make, and I took a long time to make it — five minutes that seemed like an eternity.

The cards that would save me were a J (there were two left), an 8 (four left) or a K (also four left) — 10 cards of the 44 left in the deck, or pot odds of 20%. The other thing I had to take into consideration was that I had to put in 11 million chips to win 30 million, a three to one investment; if I won the pot, I'd have a huge chip lead. Also, even though I'd be a lot weaker if I lost, I'd still have a few million chips. And remember: there was still a possibility that Matt was bluffing.

At the end of this long and difficult thought process, I decided that given the situation, the risk was worth it. I called.

When we turned over our cards before the river and I saw Affleck's pocket aces, I didn't think my chances were very good. I was pretty sure I'd lose the hand. Then the miracle happened: 8D came out on the river, which gave me a queen-high straight that beat his pocket aces. I'd just won a $41,710,000 pot and moved into the lead with a huge chip advantage.

After he lost that hand, Affleck was a sad sight to behold: he was as shell-shocked as a boxer who's just taken a right hook to the head. He hid his eyes behind his PokerStars.net ball cap, probably trying to cover up his tears. He quickly said goodbye to Joseph Cheong before leaving the table, distraught and disbelieving, and trailed by an ESPN camera. After a few minutes, he pulled himself together and came back into the room to say goodbye to his opponents.

I could've just as easily used that story in a chapter on luck, intuition, the ability to go for broke or even caution. I've used it here because it illustrates quite well the almost unbearable pressure that occurs when the stakes are high and there's no tomorrow. Without minimizing the role of luck in the hand, I also chose it to show how important it is to have nerves of steel in poker, and because I think it's full of teachable moments for someone who wants to get better at the game.

The first lesson you can take away from that story is that it's when your nerves are at their rawest that you need to rely on your self-discipline and self-control the most.

When you have difficult decisions to make, it's most important to keep your head firmly planted on your shoulders and to think clearly and logically. You may not get to choose the moment or the situations in which you're put to the test, but you still have to respond. The size of the stakes can be decisive, of course, but you can't let them take precedence over analysis.

Secondly, as I've mentioned, it's often the riskiest situations, those where one decision might cost you everything, that have the biggest payoffs. The hand I played against Affleck could've been costly for me, and it ended up being disastrous for him, but those are the hands that end up making the difference over the course of a tournament. You have to win a few of them to win the World Series of Poker.

Thirdly, when you get into a betting round, follow through or don't start in the first place. I'd already bet tens of millions of chips when Affleck went all-in on the turn. I'd have given him a gift if I'd folded at that point. I would've left the game, folding a very good hand and still pretty sure that he was bluffing. If the amount I'd invested had been my only consideration and I'd felt that he had me beat, I would've likely folded. But when I'd invested five million chips after the flop, I decided that — depending on what the next card was, of course — that I'd call the 11 million bet on the turn.

Finally, there's no room for regrets in poker. Once you've used logical reasoning and the information you have on hand to make a decision, you just have to live with it.

When you start feeling sorry for yourself, you risk going on tilt and ruining your chances, however small, in the rest of the tournament. Losing a big hand can be costly, but don't make things worse by letting your emotions get the best of you in the hands that follow. If I'd lost that hand to Affleck, for example, my stack would've dwindled to about eight million chips. Any room I'd had to breathe would've been vastly reduced, but I still would've been in the game. I still would've had the chance to make a comeback from that precarious position.

That said — and this is the last thing I'll say about this hand — my decision to call after Affleck went all-in could have gone either way. Even though things worked out in the end, I'm not sure that I'd do the same thing again under the same circumstances. My decision was based on logic, but that doesn't mean I was comfortable or confident. In fact, I was working on the premise that Affleck didn't have as strong a hand as he wanted me to think he did, but you can never be sure of something like that. It's the nature of poker — you can't avoid it.

Even though I know it's possible to question my decision, one thing's for certain: Affleck played the hand very well, raising the stakes before and after the flop, going all-in at the right moment and building his offensive attack to make it seem like he was bluffing. The proof is that I thought he was bluffing. His hand was favored to win, so he owed it to himself to bet it all. He didn't lose because he made a mistake; he lost because poker is a game in which luck has the final word.

Those kinds of situations, where your back is up against the wall, start to happen more often during the final hours of a tournament, on the final table or just before it, when there are just a few players left. It's like they say: it's at the end of the night that you know who the best dancers are. I think that also applies to poker tournaments. At the end of a tournament, stacks are big, and there's a strong temptation to eliminate players with fewer chips because every time a player disappears, those who remain see both their stacks and their chances of winning the tournament increase. But those situations can come back to haunt you. The player who's under attack has to have nerves of steel, but so does the player who's on the offensive.

Since the start of this chapter, I've been talking about situations where you're facing an opponent who's challenging you and testing your nerves. But the reverse can also cause stress. If I think I have good chances of really hurting an opponent by forcing him to put his remaining chips or the majority of his stack into play, I have to think seriously about how I'm going to do it, and whether it's a good idea. Aggressive play is usually rewarded in poker. But it requires nerves of steel. If I take my opponent head on, I have to ask myself the same questions I would if I was the one under attack.

In situations like that, avoid raising the stakes just to show off, to scare your opponent or to impress the crowd. The process of betting to raise the stakes is difficult to improvise, especially in moments that require a lot of strategy. You have to take a ton of information into consideration, from mathematical probabilities to your opponents' style to the results of previous hands. That type of play should exist within a well-considered strategy and be deployed at the right moment.

Like President Harry Truman used to say, "If you can't stand the heat, get out of the kitchen." To play high-level poker, you have to be able to withstand intense heat.

12

Caution

"You will show your poker greatness by the hands

you fold, not the hands you play." — **Dan Reed**

I'm known as a fairly aggressive player, so it may seem contradictory that caution is one of the qualities that I think every good poker player should have. It's clear to me that you can't regularly win at poker without a certain amount of restraint, without carefully weighing every decision in light of all the other information you have. Aggressive, yes. Reckless, no. It's a matter of balance.

A player who registers for a tournament thinking he'll get there, put on a show and beat everyone just by playing aggressively is likely to be disappointed. Poker is still a card game and, like I've said, most pro players only play one hand out of every four. Players don't make indiscriminate bets in high-level poker — everyone knows that a certain level of caution is necessary. You should never go to war with a pea-shooter.

During the Main Event of the 2010 WSOP, I was at the table for 10 days, and nine of those were 12-hour-plus days. When you're playing under those conditions, you have no choice but to have patience and use caution once in a while, especially at the end of the day, when exhaustion might affect your judgment. You can put all of your chips into play at any moment in a no-limit Texas Hold'em tournament. It's enormously risky — one wrong move can be fatal. In a no-limit tournament, the sword of Damocles is always hanging over your head.

Playing aggressively is one key to winning at poker, in that it allows you to throw your opponents off balance and encourages them to make mistakes. I bet or raise big and I immediately cast uncertainty in their minds. A player who has a strong hand will call and one with a weak hand will fold. The player with a medium hand — a low pair, say, or Q-10 — will hesitate because I'm asking him to make a bigger investment than he wants to make. Depending on whether he thinks I have a strong hand or I'm bluffing, he'll either call or fold. He'll pay the price if he's wrong. And if he folds, he may see cards come out on the flop, the turn or the river that would've won him the hand if he'd called.

In poker, you want to make your opponents pay for their mistakes. That means making them lose chips if they call, but it also means shutting them out of a pot by forcing them to fold earlier than they'd like. But there's a flip side to that. If you're overly aggressive, if you bet or raise big when you have a weak hand, you might get beaten at your own game. If I bluff on a non-suited 2 and 8 before the flop when my opponent has A-K, he'll call for sure. In that situation, I'll probably end up with a losing hand on the river or even earlier. That's an example of not being cautious enough.

Some players specialize in taking advantage of their opponents' lack of caution. If I'm playing against a very aggressive player, I can deprive him of the value he hopes to leverage from his bold play by responding weakly to his attacks and calling instead of raising. Not only am I minimizing his potential profits, I might also take a few hands that his over-aggressiveness cost him. That's what we call "slow play."

Let's be clear: in poker, it's much better to be aggressive than to be cautious. But if you're not cautious enough, you risk losing everything you won by playing aggressively. Don't confuse aggressiveness and carelessness. If you go on the attack, you should always watch your back. And if you bluff with a weak hand, you should know your opponents well enough to be pretty sure they'll respond passively to your attack. On the other hand, if you have a strong hand and you want them to call or raise, you have to act in a way that will allow you to get the maximum benefit from the hand. Otherwise, you risk losing a lot.

I should also underscore the following: in poker, as in other sports, the player or team that's winning at the end of a match will be more cautious and take far fewer risks than the player or the team that's behind. When Phil Mickelson leads by three strokes with five holes to go, he's not going to try to beat his record for the longest drive. He'll probably tee off with a three-wood and try to avoid making any mistakes. If, on the other hand, the Canadiens are down by two goals in the second half of the third period, they'll push their offense at the expense of their defense. Same thing happens in a poker tournament. When I got to the final table of the Main Event of the 2010 WSOP, I was the chip leader, and it wasn't in my best interests to take any risks. I owed it to myself to be cautious.

♦

Most good players try to use a minimum amount of caution. But you can always tell a beginner by their extreme cautiousness.

Most people starting to play for serious money are overly cautious, because they are afraid of losing large sums. It's an understandable reaction: being cautious is a good way to compensate for a lack of experience and an inability to properly read the game and the expected value of a hand. During that learning stage, you should choose your hands with care and limit aggressive play to strong hands. If you lack experience and you go into battle with bad cards, you'll run straight into trouble — especially if you make the mistake of playing for high stakes. During this stage, it's best to play for small sums, or with virtual money online. That way you can play as many hands as you want without losing your shirt. It's the least costly way of gaining experience and becoming a better player.

Keep in mind, though, that you can't take the cautious approach forever if you want to move forward.

I remember the first tournaments I played in Montréal, where registration costs were $200. I'd just turned 18, and my financial resources were limited. I was very nervous and cautious even though I had a lot of experience playing online. I didn't always take the necessary risks in those tournaments, and I often folded hands that I wouldn't hesitate to bet on today. I passed up opportunities that were mathematically guaranteed to win me a hand, as a lot of beginners do. I rarely bluffed and my fear stood in the way of me measuring the potential of certain hands. I wasn't taking the means necessary to maximize my profits, which is one of the fundamental goals of poker.

Imagine how I felt in October 2008 when I first participated in a tournament where the registration fee was $10,000. It was the Main Event of the World Poker Tour in Niagara Falls, Ontario. Not only did it seem like a colossal investment, but I was also going up against international poker legends like Daniel Negreanu, Gus Hansen, Erik Seidel and Barry Greenstein, to name a few. I was incredibly stressed out. My fear of losing led me to be way too cautious that time too. I didn't take enough risks, and I didn't play my best. It goes without saying that I came home empty-handed.

In the long run, with experience, you not only learn how to play more logically, but also how to manage fear, and you end up playing in a more balanced way. I can now easily forget how much I'm playing for, whether in a tournament or in cash games. I no longer struggle with that excess of caution that you absolutely have to get rid of if you want to get ahead as the stakes get higher.

In early January 2011, soon after my victory at the 2010 WSOP, I played in the PokerStars Caribbean Adventure in the Bahamas, a tournament where the registration fees were $100,000. Guy Laliberté and I were the only Quebeckers among the 38 registered players. I didn't finish well, but I played fairly aggressively. You're probably thinking I didn't have to worry too much about trying to forget the amounts that were at stake, given that I'd won millions two months prior. But a win of that magnitude doesn't make you forget the value of a dollar. I'm a middle-class kid who always worked for my spending money. I still know what $100,000 is worth. When I invested that amount in the tournament, I wasn't throwing it out the window — I wanted to see it grow.

If, after some time, the fear of losing still haunts you to the point that it prevents you from taking risks and making certain plays, there's a good chance you're not meant to play high-caliber poker. Up to a certain point, you can chalk up an excess of caution to a lack of self-confidence and a difficulty in controlling your emotions. If you bet weak, rarely raise and almost never bluff — if you're too cautious — it's because fear is limiting your ability to read the game, to think clearly and to make good decisions.

Few poker pros are known for their caution at the table, and with good reason: it's nearly impossible to win in the long term if you don't show a bit of aggressiveness. There is one exception to that rule: Dan Harrington, the great poker theoretician whose books taught me so much and who won the WSOP in 1995. Now that he's 66, you see him less often in big tournaments, but he's still a tight player who's very choosy about his starting hands. He's so cautious — at least compared to other pro players — that people jokingly call him Action Dan.

The Main Event of the WSOP is a marathon, not a sprint. Near the end of Day 2, I found myself in a situation that called for caution.

I'd been very active all day, the most aggressive player at my table. I bet with 10H-8H from the hijack, two seats to the right of the button. The big blind calls and we both see the flop, which comes out JH-6C-2H. The JH gives me a flush draw. My opponent checks.

I'm in an aggressive mood and I have a good drawing hand, so I take my chances and bet 65% of the pot. My opponent calls.

KD comes out on the turn and my opponent checks again. I could take the free card and hope to complete my flush hand but the king is a good card to bluff on, and it's still within the realm of what I could have in my hand. It'll make him think twice if he only has a pair of jacks and I'm betting strong. He also can't ignore the possibility that if I bet on the turn, I'll probably bet on the river. So I bet 65% of the pot again. He thinks for a second and calls.

3H comes out on the river and, to my great surprise, my opponent almost bets the pot. I've completed my flush, and my aggressive play could make anyone think I'd go all-in. But given the way the hand has been played so far and given my aggressive style throughout the day, it seems unlikely that he'd bluff. So, in spite of what seems like a strong hand, I decide to call. Wise choice: he flips over AH-QH for a higher flush draw! He wins the hand, but

> I can't really be disappointed given that my cautiousness allowed me to escape with only minimal losses.

♦

In this chapter, I've described how to use caution as a strategy in a game or a tournament, and I've tried to give examples of situations where it may be called for and situations where, in my opinion, it's good to be more aggressive. I now want to take the opportunity to discuss caution as it applies more broadly to poker in general.

I love poker. I'm genuinely passionate about the game. I like its competitive and strategic nature, the feeling I get when I play and the opportunities it's given me to travel around the world and meet interesting people. The goal of this book is to highlight the game's rational and logical side and to allow readers to figure out whether they have the characteristics that might allow them to win on a regular basis.

I'm lucky that I love poker and that I have most of the qualities necessary to be successful at it. However, in spite of its mathematical and strategic elements and the profit possibilities it offers, poker is still a game of chance that can be very addictive and, like drugs and alcohol, can destroy lives. Gambling addiction is a societal problem that I'm acutely aware of. I would never want this book or my personal success to encourage someone to throw themselves recklessly into the game. Poker has to remain just that: a game. A way to have fun and relax. You can't think of it as a way to make easy money. Gambling addicts usually rely solely on luck. They'll never win in the long term because they lack at least two of the qualities that are essential to success in poker: discipline and self-control. If you see yourself in that description, run as fast as you can.

That said, I encourage anyone who discovers they have a real talent for poker to develop their potential, keeping in mind that it's a long road. Working your way to the top requires patience and caution, especially when it comes to how much you're betting. It's important not to skip any steps.

13

Endurance

"I dare anybody to tell me that a tournament like the
World Series of Poker doesn't require as much if not
more physical and mental endurance as sport."

— Nolan Dalla

An activity you do while seated and barely moving
your hands might seem like the farthest thing from
a sport. But there's no doubt in my mind: poker
is definitely a sport. A mental sport, sure. It may
not require physical aptitude, but it does require a
level of endurance and concentration that's as high
as what's expected from pro athletes. One of a poker
player's greatest challenges, especially in tournament play, is to be able to keep all of his senses
functioning while sitting at a table for hours.

There are lots of links between sports and poker.
Did you know, for example, that Doyle Brunson was
set to become a pro basketball player before a leg injury
put an end to his dream? That the Finnish player Patrik
Antonius had to give up on his dream of becoming a

pro tennis player because of an injury? That several NHL players are also excellent poker players? And that, after retiring, European soccer pros Tomas Brolin, Vikash Dhorasoo and Tony Cascarino all became poker pros? Same goes for tennis legend Boris Becker and 16-time Olympic medal winner Michael Phelps.

A poker tournament — especially the Main Event of the WSOP — is like a marathon. Comprised of several days of 12-hour-plus sessions that are rarely interrupted, and then only by very short breaks, tournaments require consistency, careful attention and unflagging concentration. You can't put in a high-level performance for that long when you're not in excellent physical shape. There's no doubt in my mind that I won the 2010 World Series because of my talent and good luck, but also because my physical and mental capacities were at their best.

I know a lot of very talented poker players who've never made it to the big leagues because they get tired after a few hours at the table and lose their concentration. They are then more prone to making fatal errors. It's a common occurrence, but many players underestimate its impact. More than once, I've seen players go through long and extremely lucrative periods only to fall apart, lose everything and hate themselves for not having left the table an hour earlier. I'm still shocked at how often players fail to identify their exhaustion and pull out at the right moment.

There aren't many options for players who can't maintain their concentration for more than a few hours. They either have to learn how to quickly identify the signs of exhaustion and have the discipline to leave the table when it hits, or they have to increase their endurance so their bodies and minds can stay the course for a longer period.

The first solution is only an option during cash games, where you can get up at any moment, regardless of whether you're winning or losing. Tournaments are another matter. There you have two choices: improve your physical condition in order to increase your endurance, or stop playing tournament poker.

♣

There have been remarkable feats of endurance in the world of poker. I'll talk about two of them in this chapter.

The first one involves Viktor Blom, a 21-year-old Swedish player who made a spectacular splash in the world of online poker under the moniker Isildur1. His true identity was only revealed at the PokerStars Caribbean Adventure in January 2011 — a tournament I also played in — shortly after he joined the PokerStars team.

At 18, Blom deposited $2,000 with an online poker site and, over a few weeks, managed to increase his bankroll to almost $2 million by playing simultaneous hands of heads-up Texas Hold'em for 15 hours a day.

Isildur1 really started making waves in September 2009. Playing on a different poker site, he started taking bets from anyone who wanted to play high stakes against him. By mid-November, his bankroll was up to $6 million, earnings he won by beating well-known pros like Tom Dwan, Brian Townsend and Cole South. Then the tables turned. Isildur1 went up against Phil Ivey, considered by many to be the world's best poker player, and lost $3.2 million in a week. A few days later, he lost $3 million to Patrik Antonius in 24 hours. On December 8, he lost $4.2 million to Brian Hastings in just five hours. He set the record for total wins and losses in a single session.

In a matter of weeks, Blom played the 10 highest pots in online poker history — an incredible climb and a staggering fall. By all accounts, it was his hyper-aggressive style and his complete disregard for his bankroll that caused that rapid rise and fall. Blom himself attributed his success to his ability to stay focused during poker sessions that sometimes lasted up to 15 hours straight. And in that sense, he has a real pro's endurance.

During the fall of 2009, anyone who wanted to go up against Isildur1 could easily find him online at almost any time of day or night. His endurance is even more impressive when you realize he was playing up to six simultaneous hands while online. Playing six hands at the same time may be par for the course for many online poker players, but playing heads-up, which is what Blom was doing, requires an uncommon degree of concentration.

Some people think Viktor Blom is an aggressive show-off who won't get very far. Others believe he's a poker genius that people will be talking about for a long time yet. I played against him during the 2011 European Poker Tour in San Remo, Italy, and, in my opinion, he's unique. He plays almost every hand, bluffs constantly and bets and raises at full throttle. I was impressed by his intelligence, his daring and ingenuity in finding a win. He obviously has the endurance and other qualities necessary to do well in a tournament, but, for now, I think he lacks the patience and the caution that he'd need to go far in a competition with several thousand registrants. His style is much better suited to online cash games.

The other player who's demonstrated remarkable endurance is Phil Laak. An Irish-born American, Laak's style is aggressive and unpredictable. He has one title to his name, and he's made it to the final table of the World Poker Tour three times. On June 6, 2010, at the Bellagio in Vegas, he played for 115 consecutive hours — that's four days and 18 hours — beating the world record for endurance in poker by 37 hours. What's even more impressive is that he did it without relying on soft drinks, energy drinks or coffee. And he walked away from that marathon $10/$20 Texas Hold'em session up by $6,766!

In order to keep himself awake for that long, Laak did lots of push-ups. He'd also spent six months preparing, exercising daily and living on a diet that was heavy on carbs with a low glycemic index. He'd also lost about 26 pounds.

♣

Endurance can be defined as the ability to overcome fatigue, but it also means different things to different people. Those who can function on little sleep generally have better endurance. Genetics are also an important factor, as is age. But, as the Phil Laak example shows, it's possible to improve endurance, regardless of its natural level, by eating well and exercising. The old adage "healthy mind, healthy body" holds true.

In popular culture, the world of poker has long been associated with smoky backrooms filled with unsavory characters where the taps are always running, violence is par for the course and the smallest argument can end in a fistfight. That might have been true at some point, but it's not anymore. The world's best poker players — especially the newer generation — lead pretty ordinary lives and pay a lot of attention to staying in shape, which is tied to their mental strength and intellectual acuity.

Any high-level poker player knows that these days, talent alone isn't enough to get ahead. You have no choice but to treat your body as a pro athlete would his. Take Daniel Negreanu: he plays a lot of golf, works out every day and does yoga. He's also a vegetarian, and he avoids alcohol before a big tournament. And he's not the only one. Gus Hansen, once the Danish junior tennis champ, plays golf, squash and soccer. Patrik Antonius, one of the world's best online poker players, is a former athlete who takes physical fitness very seriously, and he considers it key to keeping his nerves in check and remaining focused over long periods of time.

Of course, there are players who rely on other methods. Excessive caffeine intake is common. But in my experience, drug abuse isn't common in the world poker.

I personally place a lot of importance on physical fitness. When I'm at home in Boucherville, I play hockey in the winter and switch to soccer, volleyball and golf in the summer. When I'm away at a tournament, I spend as much time doing laps in the pool as I can. And I try to walk from the hotel to the casino whenever possible. I don't smoke, of course, I drink in moderation and I don't consume alcohol before or during a tournament. I try to eat well all the time. I do my best to avoid red meat the day of a tournament and stick to chicken, fish, fruit and vegetables. I drink less coffee and more green tea. I eat a balanced breakfast, especially during tournaments, and light snacks that satisfy my hunger without filling me up too much throughout the rest of the day. I also try to get to sleep at a reasonable hour, a crucial practice during tournaments. It's essential to staying awake and in good shape during a long workday. That might seem like a lot, but you have to have good habits if you're going to be playing poker for 12 hours a day, seven days a week.

The 2010 World Series made me glad for all of the effort I put into maintaining a healthy lifestyle.

In the wee hours of the morning of Day 8 of the Main Event, there were only 10 players left. One of them would be eliminated to give us the final table. Play had slowed down: no one wanted to be eliminated in 10th place and bust out before the November Nine. Things carried on that way until 6 a.m. We'd been playing for 17 hours straight and everyone was exhausted. Few players were raising and no one wanted to take any big risks.

However, I didn't want to let exhaustion get the better of me, and I wanted to take advantage of the other players' listlessness. After refueling with an energy bar, I took advantage of the situation by raising and re-raising higher with every hand. It was important to me to display unflagging endurance and to keep putting pressure on the other players. By the end of the day, my stack had grown from 40 million to 66 million chips without participating in any big pots. In playing lots of marginal hands — sometimes as weak as J-3, 8-2, 4-5 — on which I didn't hesitate to raise

> pre-flop, I had to be very focused in order to avoid making mistakes and setting traps for myself.
>
> Being better prepared and having more endurance gave me an advantage over certain players who were completely exhausted. Raising on almost every hand allowed me to add to my chips without risking too much, and that helped me move on to the final table with a considerable chip advantage.

There are tons of ways you can maintain a healthy lifestyle. Everyone finds the ones that suit them best, but one thing's for certain: physical exercise, regular sleeping patterns, eating well and maintaining a healthy weight will help you do well in poker just like it would in any other sport. Regular exercise encourages good circulation and brings more oxygen to the brain in addition to optimizing performance and reducing stress. And we know now better than ever that a healthy diet is fuel for the body and has a marked effect on metabolism and endurance.

Traveling from city to city for tournaments — as I've done a lot in the past year — makes it hard to maintain a healthy lifestyle. Hotel life, long days at the poker table, restaurant meals and other distractions can draw you away from your good habits. Las Vegas, where most of the tournaments are held, isn't an ideal environment. The glamor, the shows, the jet-setting and the omnipresence of money present a host of temptations. You have to resist the siren call, and that requires unwavering motivation and discipline. But it's key to maintaining a consistently high level of performance.

14

Creativity

"Imagination is more important that knowledge."

— Albert Einstein

As Darwin wrote in his theory of evolution, species that don't adapt disappear. That theory applies to all areas of life. How many seemingly solid companies have disappeared over the past 50 years? How many long-held practices are no longer used? How many objects, common 100 years ago, are now only found in dusty attics or museums? And you'd need more than 10 fingers to count the number of objects and habits that have become a regular part of our everyday lives in the past 25 years.

In sports and business, just like in countless other fields, there are periods when we privilege certain ways of doing things over others. Habits become ingrained. They're comfortable and reassuring, and don't require a lot of effort. Then, all of a sudden, someone does things a different way and it works. Suddenly, what was once considered gospel becomes outdated.

When you stagnate, you regress. Everything is in constant evolution, including the world of sports. Talented and creative players regularly revolutionize their sport, taking it to the next level and forcing their opponents to adapt and improve their game. Think of Bernard Geoffrion's slapshot in hockey, Zinedine Zidane's exceptional ball control in soccer or the way Michael Jordan used his leaping ability to throw off the other team's defense.

It's an especially creative time in poker, and that's no accident. There have never been so many players with so much talent. As I've mentioned, online poker has not only allowed more people to play the game, it's also allowed players to play the same number of hands in a few months that their predecessors took their lifetime to work up to. There are now players in their early 20s who have as much experience as a player like Phil Hellmuth or even Doyle Brunson.

What's more, the players who've come up via the internet have an acute instinct for innovation and creativity that is sometimes lacking in older and more experienced players, who often play more predictably and along more established patterns. They end up becoming comfortable with the status quo as long as they're winning, but they also lose a significant amount of their motivation, passion and desire to win. The younger players, on the other hand, are more open and have an enormous thirst for learning and winning. They find new, untested ways to play a hand and build bluffs, constantly trying to throw off their opponents. They force other players to adapt to their style, to play off the beaten path and to develop new ways to win hands.

In the last chapter, I spoke about the phenomenal Viktor Blom, a player spawned by the internet. He came from out of nowhere at the end of 2009, when he was 19, and he has been the player who's most influenced the world of poker in the past few years. His aggressive style and his seemingly limitless ability to take risks set him apart from other players and make him very hard to read. But you don't win at poker just by being aggressive. When you've played against Blom, you realize he also has a superior intellect. His biggest strength, other than his constant and outrageous offensives, is his unpredictability and his ability to take advantage of his opponents' smallest weaknesses. His style is unique. He almost always makes the first move and forces his competitors to play defensively and adapt to his style.

American player Tom Dwan is another member of this new guard of online players. (He and Blom have had some epic face-offs.) He also has an aggressive style, and he has dominated the world's best players for months at online tables with blinds as high as $500/$1,000, winning millions before they could catch up. It's really hard to bluff Dwan; he's incredibly good at reading his opponents, whom he is constantly pushing out of their comfort zones.

♠

When I'm sitting at a poker table, my goal isn't to win the most hands — it's to take as much money or as many chips as I can from my opponents. To do that, I have to throw them off the scent and constantly cover my tracks by making moves they don't expect. For example, I'll quickly become predictable if I always bet the same amount with the same type of hand. My opponents will be able to guess what cards I have, which will make it hard for me to win any money. Similarly, if my bluffs are always built the same way, people will stop taking the bait after a while. So I have to constantly vary my strategies and reinvent myself during a game or a tournament to appear impenetrable and make sure other players can never guess what my cards are.

Of course, you don't just magically become a creative poker player. You have to know and understand the game before you can figure out what your options are and then make the right choices. Picasso learned to draw before he painted *Guernica*. Paul McCartney learned to play the guitar and other instruments before he wrote "Yesterday." After you've learned the basics, read up on the game and played a few thousand hands, you'll be able to figure out the moments where you can be more creative. Everything in good time. It's important not to skip any steps.

Once you have the knowledge and the experience, how do you use your creativity? By choosing from countless possibilities in order to attain the goal you've set out for that hand. In theory, your choices are limited: you check, you bet or you fold. If your opponent bets, you can raise. And that's where you can start making some choices and building a strategy. There are more options than it may seem. Most of your creativity will be in the size of your bets and your raises. This is especially true in no-limit Texas Hold'em, where you can bet anywhere from the minimum amount to your entire stack. You opponents will try to figure out the motivations behind any bet you make. They'll formulate some hypotheses. They'll assume that the size of your bet is linked to the strength of your hand. Or, depending on how you've behaved at the table, they'll be suspicious.

When the action's on you, you have to be able to think broadly enough to figure out which options are likely to confuse your opponents or throw them off the scent. Changing up the amounts of your bets and raises is a good way to be creative. Many things can influence that type of decision: the size of the pot and of the blinds, how the size of your bet relates to the size of your stack and those of your opponents, how big your stack will be and what kinds of bets that will permit, etc. Your opponents will consider each of these factors in an attempt to figure out your strategy. You want to get the upper hand by trying to confuse them. And if they have a hard time reading you, they won't know where they stand when your turn comes around.

Acting this way can be risky: there's always a chance that

you'll lose a lot on big bets and fail to maximize your profits on smaller bets. But it's a lucrative strategy in the long run because it casts doubts in your opponents' minds and throws them off.

♠

Once in a while, I'll watch YouTube videos of Phil Hellmuth losing to one of the younger players I mentioned before. They can be very entertaining. At 47, Phil is a legend of poker. He holds the record for most WSOP bracelets (11) and most final tables (43). He also has the third highest lifetime poker earnings. His nickname, Poker Brat, comes from his bad attitude. When he loses a big pot against younger players, he often barrages them with insults, calling them idiots and telling them they should never have bet that much with the hand they had, that they won't get far playing that way, and so on. He's being dramatic, trying to intimidate players that have less experience than him. But his insults are a reminder that those players won even though they didn't play by the book. While a single hand may not mean a lot over the course of an entire tournament, these younger players are using their creativity to come up with new ways of winning big pots.

Experience is still a big asset in poker — watch players like Doyle Brunson, Johnny Chan or Phil Hellmuth — but the problem comes when habits set in and play becomes mechanical, leaving little room for creativity. That phenomenon isn't only true of the old guard; it happens to all players. But younger players are generally more driven and imaginative, less beholden to rules others take as law, and that allows them to be more open to new ideas that sometimes lead to new and successful strategies. That's not to say that more experienced players don't also adapt and re-imagine their style. It's just that they're rarely the initiators.

Contrary to popular belief, no single poker strategy is fundamentally better than another. Some players are aggressive while others are more cautious — a bit like in chess or backgammon — but each player has his own style, his own way of deploying his arsenal and of choosing the right moments to do so. You have to base your strategy on your opponents' behavior — that's where creativity comes into play. When you're planning your strategy, deciding how much to bet and when, and figuring out when to bluff, you have to be thinking about their level of play and of thought, how aggressive they are, their betting habits, the size of their stack, their body language.

Victory sits at the end of a long and winding road. The obstacles and opportunities aren't always where you think they'll be. Other than a few basic rules, there's no foolproof system. The only real winning formula is to make the player sitting across the table from you believe that your hand is better than his, or to get him to bet a lot by convincing him that he has a good chance of beating you. There are many ways to do that, and your success will depend on your hand and on your ability to read your opponents.

In January 2011, I won the European Poker Tour's High Roller tournament in Deauville. I played a hand there that's a great example of the advantage you have when you can play creatively.

On the first day of the competition, I'm on the big blind with AD-4D. My opponent, one of the best players at the table, raises from the button. I call to see the flop.

The flop comes out KD-QS-7D. I don't want to play a big pot while out of position, so I check. My opponent bets half the pot and I call, because I figure he has a king or a queen and I don't think a raise will make him fold.

3D comes out on the turn and completes my flush draw. In that type of situation, most players would check in the hopes of getting another bet. But I want to be unpredictable.

He often has a king and I don't think he'll fold if I bet. I also figure I'll be able to better hide how strong my hand is if I bet than if I check-raise. So I bet about 50% of the pot and he calls fairly quickly.

2S comes out on the river, a card that shouldn't affect the hierarchy of hands. Given how quickly he called on the turn, I'm guessing he has a pretty strong hand. Most players in his shoes would bet in order to avoid a situation where the other player checks, thus making them miss out on an increase in the pot. At the same time, the speed with which he called on the turn could also mean that he has a very good hand and he'll think he has the better hand if I check. So I decide to be creative and I check on the river, which is a bit unorthodox. My strategy bears fruit because he bets. I get a bit dramatic and go all-in, which throws him off. After thinking it over for several minutes, he still can't figure out my hand, so he calls with K-J, never figuring that my play on a minted hand would be so logical. And he's right. My play wasn't logical, which is what allowed me to double my chips on that hand.

Poker is a sucker's game. With every new hand, you have to figure out a way to lead your opponents astray. Sometimes, you do it by faking a strong hand. Other times, you do it by pretending to be more uncertain than you are. And other times, you do it by losing a small or medium pot in order to send a false message, in the hopes that you can win a bigger pot down the road.

Players who are set in their ways are often robotic and lacking in creativity. They play perfunctory poker that guarantees them X amount of profit over Y period of time. They're not trying to get the most out of every situation by playing creatively and continually redefining their strategies. Creativity requires an open mind, a keen intellect and consistent effort. You have to be creative to make it to the top. The poker champion constantly reinvents himself by displaying a capacity for creativity that allows for unorthodox but still logical hands. His opponents know he's dangerous, but they have trouble figuring out the motives for his actions.

You can't teach creativity. It comes with a certain amount of experience. When you're making a decision, you have to imagine all the possibilities and avoid discarding any of them because they're not in the playbook. There's no superior play in poker. There are only profit possibilities based on your ability to manipulate your opponents. If you can find a way to do that, anything is possible.

15

Intuition

"Practice, practice, practice and listen to your inner voice. If you get the feeling that throwing your chips in the pot isn't a good idea, you're probably right."

— **Arthur S. Reber**

Throughout this book, I've been telling you that poker is first and foremost a game founded on logic and decisions that are carefully weighed against the benchmark of reason — a game where there's no place for emotion. And now I'm going to tell you that intuition is one of the qualities you need to have if you want to win on a regular basis. Rest assured, this will soon make sense.

Contrary to popular belief, intuition has nothing to do with premonitions, magical thinking or a sixth sense that allows you to get inside your opponent's head. It has more to do with leaning towards a certain decision without a clear idea why than it does with playing the psychic and trying to predict the unpredictable.

Intuition comes from the Latin word *intueri*, which means to pay close attention. The *Canadian Oxford Dictionary* defines it as "the power of understanding situations or people's feelings immediately, without the need for conscious reasoning or study." Basically, it refers to the information stored in your brain that you may not totally be aware of but that you take into consideration when you're making a decision.

When you think about it, it seems obvious. When you play poker, you make decisions based on facts, probabilities and incomplete information. You can be great at math, have a peerless sense of observation, be a gifted psychologist and a really lucky guy, but you still never know for sure the way a hand will end. You're always missing some piece of information that will stand in the way of you being able to properly judge a situation. Here, logic has its limits.

♥

Often, intuition comes into play in situations where the strategy seems obvious, but you somehow find yourself in doubt.

For example, suppose I have 10S-10H. I raise before the flop and my opponent re-raises. I call. The flop comes out 6D-9H-5C and he bets. I call even though I think I have the better hand and could easily raise. AH comes out on the turn and we both check. 10C on the river gives me three of a kind and my opponent bets.

My hand is strong, and nothing in this picture seems like a threat. In theory, I should raise big to increase the size of the pot. But I'm not sure that's the right thing to do. I don't know why, but even though I have a strong hand, I feel like I'm in a weak position. Even though I know my opponent's chances of winning are small, and it seems in my best interests to raise, I can't shake that doubt, for which I don't have a rational explanation.

I follow my intuition and call instead of raising, and chide myself for my lack of courage, which has made me miss an opportunity to grow my stack. My opponent turns over pocket aces, which gives him three aces. I should be surprised and even a bit disappointed, but strangely I feel reassured. My intuition was right, and it saved me a lot of chips because it made me act more cautiously.

What accounts for my decision? I'd have a hard time explaining it. I wouldn't hesitate to tell someone with a hand like mine to raise on the river. But my inner voice told me to act differently. Did I unconsciously notice something in my opponent's behavior? In how quickly he bet? Did I notice a similarity between this hand and a hand he played earlier in the day? If I could answer these questions, we'd be talking about a rational decision that I could explain, not intuition. All I know is that I wasn't comfortable with the move logic was telling me to make.

The reverse situation can also occur. I could have what seems like a weak hand — a pair of nines, say, or a low two-pair — in the face of a weak board but still feel like I could prevail.

I've learned to listen to my intuition over the years. It's not infallible, and it's sometimes caused me to make bad decisions, but it's given me more wins than losses on the whole. If I didn't listen to it, what would set me apart from a machine that's been programmed to react X way when prompted with stimulus Y? Even though computers now beat humans at chess, at backgammon and even at *Jeopardy!*, I don't think they'll measure up to the best poker players on the planet any time soon.

The inner voice that whispers in my ear doesn't come from beyond. It's not the voice of a muse. Intuition belongs in the same category as deep knowledge of the self. It's a kind of radar that scans my poker knowledge, my past experiences, the millions of hands I've played and the information and lessons I've gleaned from them. That's why I have to listen to it even though it's only an impression, a feeling, and not a complicated and educated calculation. You can definitely get better at poker by reading books, memorizing probability calculations and watching tournaments on TV. I'd even say that you have to do those things if you want to improve. But when you're playing a hand and you've done all the math, analyzed the situation and assembled all the available information, you still have to answer this important question: Does my opponent have the cards I think he has? Intuition can be very valuable in answering that question. Don't write it off because it doesn't seem like the result of a long thought process at first glance.

In a previous chapter, I compared the brain to a hard drive on which you save all the data you need to make a good decision. That data doesn't always make its way into your brain in the same way and with the same emphasis. And you're not always aware that some of that information is even there. For example, do I remember noticing that one of my opponents held his cards more tightly or closer to his chest than usual at a certain point? That another player tends to sulk almost imperceptibly when he has a weak hand? That his hands shake a bit when the stakes are high? Did I hear a sigh of satisfaction or of disappointment come from another player? Maybe not. At least, not all the time. But there's a good chance that my eyes or my ears recorded that information without me knowing it and that it's been etched into my subconscious so it can float to the surface when I need it.

Let me be blunt: beginners who rely on their intuition to win hands are asking for trouble. The reason is simple: novices have a tendency to conflate intuition with magical thinking. What they consider to be intuition is actually a strong wish for a good card to come up on the board. They rely solely on luck. True intuition, though, is a bit more complicated. It comes from experience.

The truth is that intuition comes from playing a lot of hands, identifying betting sequences, observing your opponents' attitudes and, little by little, gaining a real understanding of the game. It's only after you've accumulated that bulk of knowledge that intuition can really play a positive role in your performance.

All great pro players — from Doyle Brunson to Phil Ivey and Phil Hellmuth — admit that they rely on intuition on a regular basis. Some of them are real masters in the field. I'd be remiss if I didn't mention Daniel Negreanu here too. His acute sense of observation and his extraordinary ability to read plays and his opponents give him a definite advantage at the table. His intuition has become legendary in poker circles. He can win against very aggressive players, partly because of his self-control, and partly because of his exceptional understanding of the game and his unique ability to make the right move at the right moment. As he puts it, his subconscious has seen the movie a thousand times and it tells him what he has to do in a given situation.

When you think of it, poker and life aren't all that different. When you have an important decision to make — about a career change, say, or buying property or hiring a new staff member — you look at the pros and the cons in a logical way but, in the end, when it's time to make a decision, something else comes into play. You don't solely rely on the list of pros and cons. That little voice that speaks from the sum of your experience weighs heavy in the balance, even if you can clearly explain your motivations. That's what intuition comes down to in the end — it really has nothing to do with a roll of the dice.

Is intuition a rare gift shared by an elite minority? Not at all. Anyone can hone it. How? First, as I've mentioned, through practice and experience. When you play a lot, you end up imprinting your mind with a huge amount of knowledge on an infinite variety of plays, from the simplest to the most complex. The more hands you play, the more likely you are to recognize, whether consciously or not, certain hints or behaviors from which you can learn a lesson. In fact, you shouldn't just be sharpening your intuition while you're playing; you should also be watching other players even when you're not playing a hand.

When you don't feel pressured by risk, you're often more receptive to the flow of information around you, and you can see the game from your opponents' point of view, an asset that's essential to winning regularly at poker. When you're starting out, you can make things easier on yourself by focusing on only one player. As you get better at reading people, you can start watching more than one person at once. I'd even recommend that less experienced players do something I've often done, which is to sit down at a table online just to watch more experienced players in action. After a while, you can try to predict the results of a hand based on the observations you've collected. You'll learn a lot that way.

Intuition is not acquired from one day to the next. And you shouldn't make the mistake of relying on it before you've mastered the fundamentals of the game. But, as you become more experienced, you'll start recognizing that little voice that speaks from the information you've stored in your subconscious. It's important to remember that it's only one of many weapons in your arsenal. Don't start giving it a special role and believing it's infallible when it isn't. It replaces neither logic nor reasoning; it only completes them.

I played a hand in the preliminary round of the 2011 WSOP where my intuition had a major role.

It's early in the day of a fast tournament where the registration cost is $1,500. The skill level at my table is fairly uneven, but the game is still pretty easy. I raise with AS-QD while in medium position, and everyone folds except for the small blind, who calls. The big blind folds.

My opponent on the small blind is a man in his forties who seems to know who I am. He systematically seeks out confrontation instead of trying to avoid me. Every time I bet into a pot, he bets too, and he seems to take great satisfaction in winning pots into which I've put money.

We watch the flop come 10H-7C-4C. He checks. So do I because I figure he's going to call all my bets and I'd rather take the free card.

8H comes out on the turn and he bets. I know he may have a pair, but my intuition tells me that he doesn't have that strong a hand, that all he wants is to win against me. I follow my intuition and call his bet.

The river card is KD. My opponent quickly makes a fairly big bet.

I'm still getting the feeling that all he wants is to force me out of the pot. But he's made a big bet, and I'm not happy that a king came out on the river. My brain keeps telling me that all I have is an ace high, but my intuition tells me it could be enough to beat him. I'm pretty sure he's bluffing; his fast bet on the river, made as though the K didn't change anything, adds to my doubts.

Intuition is sometimes stronger than reason. I decide to follow my gut and call his bet. My opponent is outraged and discards face down. And I take the hand with an ace.

16

Taking Risks

"Winning at poker is all about making the right

decision." — **Phil Gordon**

In prior chapters, I recounted several hands played during the 2010 WSOP in which a player — either me or one of my opponents — made a decision that determined the course of the rest of the tournament. I'm thinking of when Joseph Cheong decided to go all-in against me before the flop with AS-7H and only three players left at the table (Chapter 8). I'm thinking too of that hand when Matt Affleck had AS-AC and I had JH-JC and I called when he went all-in with 11.6 million chips (Chapter 11).

Situations like those happen a lot in big tournaments. They call on a bunch of qualities that I've described in detail in this book, including self-control, concentration, confidence and nerves of steel. They also require you to be able to take risks.

Though those risks often happen in the final phase in the chain of events that make up a hand, they're far from a formality.

◆

As the quote at the beginning of this chapter states, poker comes down to just one thing: making the decision that will maximize your profit and minimize your losses. It seems simpler than it really is though, mostly because the more you move up the ranks, the more you start to realize that the decision-making process relies heavily on a considerable number of unpredictable factors. There are strong probabilities, sure, but no guarantees. There's always a risk, and it can sometimes be quite high. But in the end, once you've analyzed the available information and made your calculations, you just have to go for it. The higher the stakes — like when you're getting close to the final table of a tournament — the harder it can be to make a decision.

There are four betting rounds during a hand of Texas Hold'em: before and after the flop, on the turn and on the river. Players can choose to check, call, bet, raise (and re-raise) or fold at each round. In each situation, the decision to call, bet or raise can have serious consequences. In fact, both in online cash games and during a tournament, the size of the pot can grow to become fairly large even before the flop. Even if you just go for a round of betting with two good cards in your hand and without considering the size of your stack, your position at the table or the caliber of your opponents, it'll still take you a while to make a decision.

Some beginners think pre-flop bets aren't very risky. That's only true if the bets stay small. But if a player who has a high pair or two high cards decides to jack up the stakes right away, you should think twice before engaging because you might end up having to bet a lot more than you wanted to see the flop.

Since the progression of bets over four rounds of betting can become almost exponential, a small variation in the amount of a pre-flop bet can result in large sums on the river. While a pre-flop re-raise may seem to have little impact, since the average bet usually varies between a third of the pot and the full amount, it can lead to a bet that's twice as big on the river.

In poker, making a decision is never a formality. Decisions can't be reduced to a mathematical formula from which there is only one answer. On the contrary: decisions are often subjective. My opponents' job is to force me to make difficult decisions.

When you're frequently faced with dilemmas to which there are several answers, you have to be able to make those tough decisions. You have to be able to identify every advantage, however minor, that one option has over another. A decision that involves a profit possibility of one percentage point over another can make a big difference in the long run, even if it seems insignificant in the moment. The profitability of a decision may seem negligible in the short term, but it never stays that way when you consider it in a long-term context. And it's in the long term where the difference between talent and chance makes itself known.

Taking risks also means being able to make tough decisions while keeping in mind the bigger picture that exists beyond the mathematical possibilities of the hand being played. Two different hands may offer similar profit possibilities in the present, but the consequences of your choice can affect your position in the larger tournament. Trying to imagine the impact of a potential outcome on the rest of the tournament can open up a hidden opportunity for profit, and suddenly make a tight decision, regardless of the direction, more logical. That's exactly what happened in that hand I played against Matt Affleck. Math wasn't helping me with my decision, and my analysis of the hand at the moment I was playing said that folding and calling offered the same potential for a win. But when I pictured the outcome of both decisions, I knew that if I folded, I'd stay in the same lead pack, while if I called, there were two possible results.

If I lost the hand, I'd still have a pretty good chance of making it to the final table and making a comeback. My position would be precarious, but not critical. If I called and won, I'd have a huge chip advantage, as well as all of the other advantages that come with that position. So, while both decisions seemed mathematically equal — even though that would no longer be the case once we showed our cards — it was the opportunity to take the lead in the tournament that motivated the decision I made.

The poker player is always on the razor's edge: he has to make decisions that may cost him most of his chips, eliminate him from a tournament or, on the flip side, give him a huge chip lead. Those decisions require clear-headedness, sound analytical skills and, often, a big dose of courage.

> **ACCORDING TO JONATHAN:** "To be able to make those tough decisions, you need the perfect balance between several personality traits, including a good understanding of who you are and confidence in your abilities. That's what'll help you get past that final, most difficult step."

♦

The ability to take risks in poker depends first and foremost on an analysis of all the information that can help you make considered and lucrative decisions. There are lots of those items, both objective and subjective. This isn't an exhaustive list, but here are the ones I think are the most important:

1. Your opponents

This is where it all starts, because every decision you make is based on the person that's sitting in front of you. Within about an hour, I can usually get a good read on my opponents. I know who plays tight, who's aggressive and how aggressive they are, the ratio of hands a particular player plays, etc. Those clues are invaluable because they tell you how far you can take your bets, raises and bluffs, and who might get in your way.

2. The size of the stacks

Every time the dealer shuffles, you have to check how many chips your opponents have. You should always be on top of that information. It's vital because it tells you how much they'll be able to intimidate you, how much they can raise and, depending on the size of your own stack, how vulnerable you are to an attack. For example, if you can't invest very much in a hand but one of your opponents has a very deep stack, you should probably fold right away. However, you should also be careful around players with small stacks who are more likely to go all-in on big pots.

3. The number of players at the table

This will influence how aggressively you play. The more players there are at the table, the likelier it is that one of them will have a big hand that can beat your pair of jacks. If there are only two or three players on a hand, there's a greater chance that your jacks will win.

4. Table position

If you're the last player to act on a hand, you have access to a lot more information than if you were the first to act. You know who folded, who bet, who raised and by how much, and you know the value of the pot. If you're in a good position, you can play more aggressively. If you're in a weaker position, you should play more cautiously.

5. How the game is playing out

Throughout a game, I'm watching the other players' betting habits, how quickly they make decisions, the expression on their faces, how their hands move, the tics and the tells that I try to match up with a certain type of hand. I want to know who's winning, who's losing, who's happy and who's frustrated, and why they're playing a certain way. Table dynamics reveal a lot of information that you can use to your advantage when you're making a decision.

6. The strength of your hand
After you get a handle on what's happening at the table, you'll have a better idea of whether you have a good hand, and you can decide if you want to invest in a hand and, if so, how much.

7. The board
You have to be able to properly read the cards that are shared among all players and that will complete your hand. Understanding them and what your outs are will give you an idea of whether you have a winning hand. The board can also help you get a better idea of what cards your opponents might have. Then, taking the other information you have into consideration, you can establish a plan of action and make the best decision possible.

8. The pot odds
As discussed in Chapter 3, pot odds are the relationship between the amount of money you need to call a bet and the amount that's in the pot. Generally, if the bet is small and the pot is big, it's worth the investment. On the other hand, if the bet is big and the pot is small, you're better off folding, unless you have a very strong hand. In other words, it's about figuring out if your hand is worth playing based on the information that's there.

♦

In poker, good decisions sometimes turn out badly, and bad decisions sometimes end up paying off. That's just how it goes.

You can't control the cards — that element of risk is what makes the game so exciting. When you're at the point where there's no turning back, lots of things are still unknown, and luck will always have the final word. But you can't dwell on that because if you do, you'll end up keeping yourself from thinking clearly and objectively. It's by making the right decisions that you'll win in the long term.

If you think you should call a large bet that could jeopardize your chances in the tournament, but folding also seems like a logical decision, though maybe not as good as calling, will you have the courage to take the risk? If you're bluffing and find yourself forced to three-bet on the river or be eliminated from the tournament, will you have the guts to do it without losing your composure? When you think of it that way, the ability to take risks is a kind of self-confidence that itself can encourage decision-making.

♦

Once you've analyzed every available bit of information, the next step is to make a decision. As I've said, it's not always easy. There are all kinds of pressures in such a situation, and they're not all just related to a fear of losing.

For example, the pressure becomes way more intense when you're playing in a televised tournament. I felt that pressure when the ESPN cameras entered the room just before the final table during the 2010 WSOP. My fear of making a mistake increased tenfold because I knew my every move was now being watched, anticipated, commented on and recorded. An error made in a small group can have serious consequences, but make it in the presence of TV cameras and suddenly it's not just a fear of losing, it's also a fear of ridicule and a fear of being judged on a single decision and being considered a bad player by millions of people.

You have to ignore those extraneous elements when you're in that situation and focus solely and objectively on what will help you make a decision, and on evaluating the information around you. That's the only way you'll be able to make the best decisions and win on a regular basis.

17

Luck

"If there weren't luck involved, I would win every

time." — **Phil Hellmuth**

When I think back to the long journey that culminated in my win at the Main Event of the 2010 WSOP, I can't help but think about how lucky I was.

I often think about a few hands I played well into the tournament. One of them was on Day 7 of the Main Event against Robert Pisano, who ended up placing 23rd. I went all-in with AH-KC against his pair of sixes. The flop came out 7D-3C-JH. When the turn brought 5C, my chances of winning the hand were only 14%. Then the KH came out on the river, allowing me, at the very last moment, to double my stack with a pot of 3.6 million chips. The same day, I had a pair of eights against Matthew Berkley's 10D-6D. A 6S-6H-3D flop gave Berkley three of a kind and gave me less than a 10% chance of winning the hand. The 8D on the turn gave me a full house and made me a favorite. After Berkley bet, I went all-in and he called. The 2C on the river didn't change anything and I got my hands on a pot of almost eight million chips.

I was also very lucky at the final table against Michael Mizrachi, at a point where there were only five of us left. He went all-in with 3D-3H and I called with AS-9H. With 54 million chips in the pot, our chances were almost even. The stakes were enormous. I remember telling Mizrachi before the flop that I wasn't too happy with the situation I was in. As though to prove me wrong, the flop came out 9D-5D-KH. My pair of nines gave me a better chance of winning, but all Mizrachi needed was another three to take it. 9C came out on the turn, which gave me three of a kind but didn't change much otherwise, given that Mizrachi could still win if he got one of the two remaining threes. Lucky for me, it was JH that fell on the river.

You can't win a high-profile tournament like the WSOP without a good amount of luck. Every high-level player will agree. And it's not enough just to be lucky: you have to carry that luck with you well into the tournament, just like I did in 2010.

Since the beginning of this book, I've told you about all the logical elements that will help you to win in the long term. But luck and chance also play a big role in high-level competitions where all the players are at about an equal skill level. Luck and chance have the final say in many hands. Often the card that you need, or the one that will make the other guy win, will come out on the river, even though the probability of that happening is less than 10%.

How much of a role does luck have in games of strategy like dice or cards? Hard to say. In backgammon, some say it's about a third, while the remaining two thirds are made up of talent, technique and the strategy with which you deploy your playing pieces. The major difference is that in backgammon, all you have to do is look at the position of the pieces on the board to know where you sit. The only unknown is what the dice will say. You can't fool your opponent into thinking you're ahead of him. In poker you can. That psychological play is part of the game, and it's one of the things that sets it apart and makes it so fascinating.

What backgammon and poker do have in common is that with a bit of luck, a novice player can beat the best player in the world for a whole night.

I've often stressed how important it is to think long term in poker. It's impossible to survive in the world of poker if you're always just thinking of the next step. You have to consider the role of luck in that same light, whether in poker or in backgammon. Why? Because while luck may prevail in the short term, it's talent and strategy that will prevail in the long term.

Let's use a simple example to illustrate this point. Say I throw a coin in the air. There's a 50% chance it'll come up tails. The results are strictly governed by chance. If I throw the coin 10 times, a variance will come into play and, while the results will still be close to 50%, it's possible — though not probable — that the coin will come up heads or tails 90% or 100% of the time. Now, let's say I throw that same coin a thousand times. The results will be in the 40% to 60% range. If I throw it one million times, the range will be even narrower, probably between 48% and 52%. That's what we're referring to when we talk about probability calculations. It's something every poker and backgammon player has to take into consideration before making a decision.

In poker, it means that if you play only one hand, luck will play a major role in the results. If you play all day, the role of luck will be reduced, but it will still be significant. Luck also remains an important factor in the results of a tournament. But if you play poker against the same players for a year, five years or ten years, luck will end up being marginal in the grand scheme

Luck

of things. You'll have runs where luck will be on your side and others when you're sure you have no luck at all. But on the whole, over a long period of time, it's talent, the ability to read the game and your tactical abilities that'll make you a winner or a loser. Luck doesn't impact your overall balance sheet. That's why you shouldn't let losing streaks get you down, however long they may last. They're normal, and every player goes through them, even the best players on the planet.

Even if probability says you have a good chance of completing a straight draw or a flush draw, the card you want doesn't always come out. But if you calculate your odds over the long run, you know you'll be a winner regardless of whether you're lucky or not.

Friends and family often call or send emails and text messages to wish me good luck before a tournament. And I know I need it. But what I want, first and foremost, is to play well. The reason is obvious: it's the only element of the game that I can control. I can't control luck, but I can make sure that I'm in good physical and psychological shape when I get to the tournament, that my senses are sharp and that I'm prepared to make the best decisions possible. Here again the similarities with everyday life are obvious. There are lots of things in life that you can't control. The important thing is to concentrate and to act on the things you can.

Still, I have to be aware of how different types of luck can affect my game and my opponents' game too. I have to maximize the profits from my win streaks and minimize the losses I incur during downswings. For example, if my opponents think I'm on a winning streak, it goes without saying that they'll fear me. They'll have more respect for my bets and raises, and my bluffs will be more successful.

You have to take advantage of the moments when luck is being good to you to max out your winnings. Go on the offense, challenge your opponents to grow the pot, especially before the flop. You have to find ways to make your opponents bet as many chips as possible without scaring them away with high raises. Therein lies much of the artistry of poker. It's not something you can master in a couple of days, but the more you play, the better you'll be able to read the table, figure out your opponents and manipulate them.

And then there are the times in a poker player's life when nothing works like it should. I complete a queen-high straight draw and my opponent has the same straight, but his is king or ace high. I have a jack-high full house and my opponent has one with kings, or four of a kind. When you're in a bad place, remember that your opponents can tell, and that they will try to intimidate you by betting big. So you want to become more controlled, to play more tightly, because winning players are inspired, and inspired players always play better. That's especially true in a situation where you're the target. You have to remain cautious in those situations. It's not the time to take on the table.

If you're playing cash games, it's not a bad idea during those kinds of runs to set yourself a loss limit and be disciplined enough to play by it. It's a well-documented fact that a player on a losing streak has a tendency to want to win his money back. You'll want to do it fast too, and that's often when disaster hits. You're impatient, you bet too much, take unnecessary risks and end up making the situation worse. You have to be humble and clear-headed enough to admit defeat. After all, there'll be lots of opportunities to redeem yourself.

You can have all the talent in the world, but you still need luck to become the world champion. What you have to remember is that in poker, as in all other games of chance, the overall winners are the players who play well, not the ones who are lucky.

Luck

Luck doesn't only show up during televised moments of high drama, as was the case during my hand against Matt Affleck. The best example I can think of happened during Day 5 of the 2010 WSOP. At that point, my stack was less than 10 times the big blind, and things weren't looking good for me.

I get A-5 in late position. The size of my stack limits my options, so I have no choice but to go all-in to try to steal the blinds and the antes, which, when added up, would allow me to increase my stack by 25%. I go all-in and the big blind calls with A-10. My tournament life is suddenly in jeopardy: my chances of survival are less than 30%.

But Lady Luck smiles on me: A-5 turns up on the board, I win the hand and I double my chips. The hand was fairly innocuous on the whole, but it's one of those hands that can help you win a long tournament. I was lucky to win a bunch of them during the 2010 WSOP. If luck hadn't been by my side during moments like that, you wouldn't be holding this book in your hands.

18

Experience

"If it weren't for online poker, many of the best next-generation players wouldn't measure up to the more experienced players. Thanks to it though, you can acquire several years worth of experience in a few weeks." — **John Tabatabai**

When you think of experienced poker players, you think of Doyle Brunson. Nicknamed the Godfather of Poker, the 78-year-old has had a very successful career: almost $6 million in winnings, 10 WSOP bracelets and back-to-back victories at the WSOP Main Event in 1976 and 1977. Over his 50-plus-year career, the living legend has played against the best players of the last half-century, from Chip Reese and Stu Ungar to Daniel Negreanu and Phil Ivey. These days, he plays in fewer tournaments than he used to, but he's still a formidable opponent, in spite of his age.

Like many great players, Doyle Brunson's story began with a reversal of fortune, back when the poker world was still largely synonymous with violence — when it wasn't uncommon for pro players to be taken for their winnings at gunpoint after a game. For six years, Brunson teamed up with pals Amarillo Slim and Sailor Roberts in cash games all over the southwestern states. They pooled their winnings — more than $100,000, all told — but lost it all the first time they went to Vegas. It was after that disastrous trip that Brunson started to build his reputation through practice and experience.

There's no doubt that you need experience to win at poker. You can pick up the mathematical side of the game — pot odds, probability calculations, profit possibilities — fairly easily early on, but it takes more time to hone a comprehensive understanding of the game and the discipline, the sense of observation, the psychology and the intuition you need to win on a regular basis.

♠

If experience plays such a big role in the game, how do you account for young guns like Viktor Blom and Tom Dwan who hold court with the best in high stakes games? And how do you explain the fact that Peter Eastgate, Joe Cada and I, also all in our early 20s, have won the WSOP for the last three years running? The answer is simple: the internet.

I was born in 1987 and grew up with the internet, so it's hard for me to measure the impact it's had on our daily lives. I have a hard time imagining a world without email, text messages, Facebook and Twitter. But I know that not that long ago, the only phones were on landlines, that to send someone a message, you had to take a pencil, write it on a piece of paper, put the paper in an envelope, put a stamp on it and put it in a mailbox.

When I play online poker, my virtual opponents are in France, Russia, Germany and Australia. We're playing in real time, and it seems normal. But I know it would have been unfathomable the year I was born. The internet has sped up life, collapsed distances and opened up access to knowledge that had previously been accessible only to the few. Poker too has been democratized with lightning speed.

What counts in poker is how many hands you've played. And, in that sense, younger online players have a lot more experience than most people might think. It's easy to prove.

Before you could play online, the only way to gain experience was to go to a casino — an activity that wasn't always an option for your average guy — or to belong to a network of aficionados who would regularly meet up to play their favorite game. In both cases, you could rarely play more than 25 hands an hour. Which means it took years to become an experienced player. On the internet, however, you can easily play eight simultaneous hands, which adds up to about 500 hands an hour. If you're playing between 40 and 60 hours a week, you're playing a huge number of hands, and gaining a lot of experience in very little time.

It's true that online players don't have that tournament experience, where you go up against flesh-and-blood opponents and collect different types of information from them, and where the psychological side of the game is more complicated. But when I'm playing 12 different tables for hours at a time on PokerStars .net, I see a huge number of different situations, and the strategic experience I acquire there is invaluable.

There are also different brands of statistical software that can record data from each hand I play. Those tools allow me to go back and analyze my plays during study sessions that happen away from the table. The software also collects data about my opponents that's sent to me in real time. That allows me to match numbers with abstractions, and to justify most of my decisions by basing them on tangible facts and stats compiled over hundreds of thousands of hands. The learning process and the way to behave around poker players with defined profiles become easier. It's a powerful asset that the old guard never dreamed of, and that's available to anyone who's playing online.

I'm not arguing with the fact that a hand played at a casino can teach me more about strategy than a hand played online, but I know that an hour spent playing online will help me improve more quickly than an hour spent playing at the casino. I also know that there's no way I would have had the experience I needed to win the WSOP at 23 if I'd only played at real tables during the five preceding years. And I know the same is true for Peter Eastgate and Joe Cada.

At 24, I'm as, if not more, experienced, than a 50-year-old player who's spent every day of the past 20 years playing in a casino. And it's not just me. There are thousands of other players like me. We're the reason poker is as popular and as competitive as it is today all over the world.

> **ACCORDING TO JONATHAN:** "In my opinion, experience has more to do with how many hours you've played than how many years you've been playing. The first step to self-realization is knowing your strengths. To stay on the road to success, you have to do everything you can to help them grow."

This ability to acquire experience so quickly is unique in the world of sports. It's as if a 20-year-old NHL rookie knew right off the bat all the tricks of the trade that a veteran player had spent 10 or 15 years perfecting. It's as if every year, every professional sport saw an influx of Wayne Gretzkys, Babe Ruths, Michael Jordans and Roger Federers.

The fact that at 25 Tom Dwan has played three times as many hands as Doyle Brunson has at 80 puts a lot of pressure on the older guard. The Phil Hellmuths, Johnny Chans and Scotty Nguyens are now up against a pack of hungry young wolves with sharp teeth who have the experience necessary to play at the highest levels of international poker.

The young generation of players is an undeniable presence not only online but also at all the high-profile tournaments. What's the proof? Seven of the nine players who made it to the final table of the Main Event of the 2011 WSOP were under 27. The Ukrainian player Anton Makievskyi and the British player Samuel Holden were 21 and 22 respectively. The majority of the players at the final table got the bulk of their experience online. It's also interesting to note that the players who made up the November Nine in 2011 came from seven different countries. In 2010, only three countries — the U.S., Canada and Italy — were represented. It's a sign that poker is no longer the dominion of a single country. And that democratization of the game is largely due to the internet.

Conclusion

On July 12, 2011, at the Rio Las Vegas Hotel and Casino, I was eliminated from the Main Event of the 2011 WSOP as I attempted to defend my title. While I outlasted the vast majority of my opponents, I didn't make it past the bubble. Afterwards, I was asked repeatedly whether I was disappointed by the outcome. Sure, I would've loved to repeat my 2010 win, or to at least have made it to the final table for a second consecutive year. But I knew right from the start that with more than 6,800 players registered in the tournament, the law of averages wasn't in my favor. Winning a poker tournament requires a delicate balance of chance, strategy and timing. I did the best I could with what I had to work with, but the stars just weren't aligned that year. It's rare that they would be two years in a row in an event of that magnitude. That said, I think I held my own during the 25 tournaments I played during the 2011 WSOP. I placed in the money in two of them, and, coming out of it, my confidence wasn't at all shaken.

With time and experience, you learn to take your losses with a grain of salt. Like they say, you can't win 'em all. That's especially true in poker, and even more so in tournament play, where you generally lose nine out of 10 times.

In December 2011, I lived through a brutal example of life's tendency to throw you curveballs when you least expect them. During the holidays, I was back at home with friends and family, enjoying a well-earned break after a very busy year. On December 21, a man dressed as a courier rang my doorbell, which didn't seem at all out of the ordinary, given the fact that I was waiting for the delivery of several gifts I'd bought online. I opened the door without a second thought. Before I could react, I was attacked by two large men. I tried to fight back, but they overpowered me. They forced me to open my safe and took everything in it. Then they tied me up and continued to beat me even though they had everything they wanted. When they were done, they took off with a large amount of cash, the Rolex watch PokerStars gave me when I was declared 2010 WSOP champion and my championship bracelet.

The police did an amazing job with the case. They discovered that a former girlfriend of mine had probably played a key role in planning the break-in. I got part of the money back, as well as the Rolex and what was left of the championship bracelet. The latter was picked up randomly by a cleaning truck in Montréal. Only a small part of the original bracelet remains, but getting it back meant a lot to me because it has such symbolic value. As I write this, I'm still waiting for the accused to go to trial. I trust in the justice system to see the case through. The whole thing is just a memory now, a page in the history books that I hope to turn for good.

The weeks that followed the attack were difficult for me. Having my personal safety breached in my own home made me feel vulnerable in a way I'd never really considered possible. I had to find ways to access stores of energy I didn't know I had in order to keep my head above water and be able to bounce back to my regular routine . . . and I say that knowing that my lifestyle is far from normal!

Throughout this book, I've tried to draw parallels between poker and life, to show that the qualities you need to excel in poker can also be applied more generally to the rest of your life, even in areas that seem diametrically opposite to the game. When I look back on the attack, those parallels seem truer than ever. I had to use every quality described in this book in order to regain my confidence at the table and to manage my psychological and physical recovery.

That brings us to early 2012 and the PokerStars Caribbean Adventure, which I was very excited to participate in. I needed to prove to myself that I was stronger than the scars left by my ordeal. What doesn't kill you makes you stronger, and I had every intention of being living proof of that. Thus the 2012 PCA was different than any other tournament I'd ever played in. The stakes went way beyond my opponents or the money. I was playing against myself, against what I'd been through and what I wanted to become.

I know that my thirst for victory was at the root of the excellent performances I put in during the tournament. Over five tournaments, I made it to four final tables, registering one win and one second-place finish. Pretty impressive, when you consider the median success rate of the average poker player. I made about $1.2 million in a week. More than the money though, that string of successes helped me get back on pace, stronger and more confident than ever.

The past few years have definitely been the best I've ever had. When I think back on this time, I feel an intense sense of satisfaction and gratitude. Between the 2010 WSOP and the upcoming

2012 tournament, I've been able to play poker all over the world from North America to Europe and Asia, to meet interesting people I would never have otherwise met, and to associate myself with charities I'm extremely proud of. In fact, I'm about to register for the historic $1 million buy-in event at the 2012 WSOP, where $111,111 from each player's buy-in will be donated to One Drop, the charity Guy Laliberté founded whose aim is to increase worldwide access to safe drinking water. I'm a spokesperson for the foundation, and I hope to be able to promote it throughout the poker community. All the professional and personal experiences I had over the course of that magnificent year of 2011 helped me become more mature and a better, more complete person who's more sensitive to the realities of the world.

My professional goal is to keep studying and to take every opportunity to maximize my potential and become the best player I can be. I've always dreamed of being able to participate in high-profile tournaments, and now I can. I'm also planning to broaden my horizons by becoming better at other poker variations, including Omaha, seven-card stud, razz, H.O.R.S.E. and 8-game. I think it'll help me be a more well-rounded and versatile player than if I only play Texas Hold'em, as I've done up until now.

I also plan to continue to be an ambassador for the game wherever I find myself in the world. I took a lot of pride in that responsibility in 2011, and I think people still expect it of me. I really believe that poker is a noble activity and that, as I've shown in this book, it calls on qualities that you need in order to be successful in many areas of life.

In closing, I hope this book will help to promote poker to skilled players and to discourage those who don't have the qualities necessary to play it. The game should always be a source of pleasure and self-fulfillment, never of anxiety and regret.

Boucherville, March 2012

Acknowledgments

I owe much of my success to the luck of having the qualities discussed in this book, but also to many people I care about. I can't ignore the immense contributions so many have made, be it in my pursuit of the WSOP title, in the adventures that followed my win, in the writing of this book or simply in my life in general.

I'd first like to thank my family for their love, for the values they instilled in me and for their constant support. They're the reason I am who I am today, and the reason I've been able to experience the extraordinary things that have happened to me. I can't stress enough how important they've been and continue to be in my life.

I also want to thank my close friends: those who were there, who are here and who will continue to be here. I think of all the good times we've had, of our shared love of poker and of all the memorable games whose stories, such a precious gift, will remain etched in my memory. I'll always remember that it all started with you. The passion I've shared in this book would never have been as strong and pure if it weren't for those lucky moments that we experienced together. That passion has become a valuable asset, and you are its soul and its inspiration.

Thanks to the many Quebeckers who came to Las Vegas, who helped motivate me and who contributed to the magic and intensity of those historic moments. Deep down, I know that without you, this unforgettable adventure never would have been so memorable.

Thanks to my sponsor, PokerStars, for the confidence you've had in me. I'm proud to be a member of the biggest poker site in the world, one with so much integrity, and one where the members share a family spirit.

Special thanks to Guy Laliberté, who didn't hesitate for even a second before agreeing to write the foreword to this book. I already had a huge amount of respect for him, and it only grew when we met. Guy is an example of the Quebec brand of perseverance and success, and he's an inspiration to me.

I'd also like to thank my agents, Yves Bouchard and Philippe Jetté of Poker Solution (www.poker-solution.com), for their helpful advice and all the time they put into making my life easier. Without them, none of what has happened in the last year would've been possible.

I'm also grateful to Martin Lalonde, M.B.A., C.F.A., and Les Investissements Rivemont for sharing his expertise in managing my finances and especially for his personal approach and his loyalty.

Thanks to PrincePoker (www.princepoker.com) for covering all of the Quebeckers who played in the 2010 and 2011 WSOP. Their team greatly contributed to my visibility, and they continue to pursue their work of increasing the media exposure of Québécois poker players.

Finally, I'd like to thank Serge Rivest and the team at Editions de l'Homme for making this book a reality. I'm lucky to have been able to take advantage of Serge's sharp mind and experienced pen, and to have been surrounded by a professional team who made every effort to bring this project to fruition.

Thanks to all of you! One way or another, you were all instrumental in helping me to achieve my dreams.

At ECW Press, we want you to enjoy this book in whatever format you like, whenever you like. Leave your print book at home and take the eBook to go! Purchase the print edition and receive the eBook free. Just send an email to ebook@ecwpress.com and include:

- the book title
- the name of the store where you purchased it
- your receipt number
- your preference of file type: PDF or ePub?

A real person will respond to your email with your eBook attached. And thanks for supporting an independently owned Canadian publisher with your purchase!